My Humor Heritage

in

Madison County
and
Beyond

My Humor Heritage

in

Madison County
and
Beyond

A. E. Ponder

<u>YAV Publications</u>
Asheville, North Carolina

Copyright © 2017 by Anthony E. Ponder

All rights reserved. No part of this book shall be reproduced or transmitted in any form or by any means, electronic, mechanical, magnetic, photographic including photo-copying, recording, or by any information storage and retrieval system, without prior written permission of the publisher. No patent liability is assumed with respect to the use of the information contained herein. Although every precaution has been taken in the preparation of this book, the publisher and author assume no responsibility for errors or omissions. Neither is any liability assumed for damages resulting from the use of the information contained herein.

Illustrations by A. Graham Ponder

First Edition

ISBN: 978-1-937449-33-9

Published by

YAV Publications
Asheville, North Carolina

YAV books may be purchased in bulk for educational, business, fund-raising, or sales promotional use. For information, contact Books@yav.com or phone toll-free 888-693-9365.

Visit our website: www.InterestingWriting.com

3 5 7 9 10 8 6 4 2

Published April 2017

Printed and Assembled in the United States of America

I would like to dedicate this work to my older sister, Audrey P. Tolison. Throughout my formative years she was my best friend, financial backer, and mentor. Best of all was her friendly demeanor, pleasing personality, and willingness to share humor with me. So Audrey, from a tag-along brother, thanks for those fond memories.

Contents

Acknowledgments ix

Introduction 1

Colonial Period..15

Founding Fathers 19

The Minstrel Show 41

Vaudeville Forward 49

Humor Heritage Local...99

Afterword 159

Acknowledgments

A few years ago I performed one of my original songs at an annual extended family gathering. So nervous was I that to loosen up from stage fright, I told a few jokes before I sang. Evidently the song wasn't too well received but my wife's niece, Sherry Lewis, suggested that I do stand-up comedy. From that humble beginning in September 2013, I have pieced together the following work that I hope you will enjoy reading as much as I enjoyed putting it together. If not, you may have purchased a good sleeping aid.

I want to thank my neglected wife, Glennis, for enduring the long hours spent on this project. I wish to thank the late Milton Berle who provided advice, guidance, and how-to with his works on humor that were published and left for us. And I want to thank the internet for the wealth of wisdom that would have been totally unavailable only a few years ago. Also, thank goodness for computer spell check.

I wish to thank the Madison County Genealogical Society. They permitted me to perform part of the contents of Humor Heritage found in the pages herein at one of their meetings. Their response and patience have allowed me to get a feel for how a work of this genre might be received by a wider audience. By their reaction I also obtained the feel for how humor has changed over the past fifty years.

Let me also thank Madison County News-Record Digital and all the folks who worked so diligently to put it together. By using those old newspapers, I was able to lead into my subject without shocking my genealogical friends and potential readers. Humor has indeed changed over the past fifty years to become more rigid as though it were being guided by a subtle, invisible hand. Perhaps, as you peruse these pages, you will notice some of these subtle and not so subtle shifts in our humor that have taken place over the past few years. I will not spell out those changes, but it is my desire to present enough information for you to discover them for yourself. Also, it is my hope that these pages will provide you with a pleasant experience.

I would like to thank A. Graham Ponder for drawing the cartoons for this work.

Oh! And lastly, I wish to thank my publisher, YAV Publications and editor, Christopher Yavelow. His timely suggestions, advice, and guidance have been invaluable. A million thanks, Chris.

Introduction

Madam Chairman Hamilton, program director King, guests, and members of the Madison County Genealogical Society, thank you for allowing me to present part one of a three part series on my humor heritage. A couple of years ago I was sitting around thinking how I could best spend my second childhood. I thought; why not try something like humor heritage. So, I want to make this a program you won't forget, and heaven knows you'll try.

Doris, all men are alike. They lose their immaturity somewhere in their second childhood.

Humor has changed a lot in the past fifty years. It has changed so much that I searched to find a way to make a smooth transition into my subject without offending you. I found what I thought was the solution to my dilemma, News-Record Digital.

Here from News-Record Digital is an article dated May 3, 1922, page five. Headline and story: "Madison County is Maintaining Time Honored Custom of Attending Court. From colonial days court week has been a gala week with America's rural population. That is the week that everybody wants to go 'to town'. While the occasion has lost many of its frills and some of its thrills such as the 'medicine man' with his snake, gas torch and much mouth gas, auction sales, horse swapping and other such pastimes, still court week is a gala week for many people, especially in remoter and rural sections of the country.

"Madison County citizenry still maintain the time honored customs of court week. They come in great numbers to the school of justice. And it is said to be good that the people get such a course in true Americanism as the court gives.

"Because of the large docket, court this week has brought large numbers of Madison's yeomanry to town. The crowd around the courthouse have more the appearance of a camp meeting than anything else. A more orderly group of people could not be found anywhere."

The article goes on to give the names of the presiding judge, solicitor, and the court docket.

As a way of getting into my subject, I want to use some short clips known as fillers. They were placed in those old News-Records to fill out the page to keep it from looking like a jack-o-lantern. Those used are sorted under the headings of mechanical, family, and ethnic. Can you hear me all right? I used to work for the government, and I tend to mumble. Let me rephrase that because "work" is a little strong. I was once on a government payroll. If they had furnished me with a car, I could have taken everybody for one big ride. These are some of the News-Record fillers from 1913–1940.

Starting with family here are a few of those fillers.

> "Okay buddy, what caused this accident?"
> "Well officer, my mother-in-law fell asleep in the back seat."

> A woman in rags appears at a front door in suburbia.
> She says: "Do you have anything you can give me? I have three husbands to support."
> The home owner says, "What are you, a bigamist?"
> The lady beggar replies: "No sir. One is mine and the others belong to my daughters."

> Have you heard about these new machines that can tell if a man is lying?
> You better believe it, I married one.

> "Give me a round trip ticket quick, I've got to catch this train."
> "All right, where to?"
> "Why, back here. Where did you think?"

> A man runs after a train and walks back into the station.
> "Were you trying to catch that train, sir?"
> "No. I was just chasing it out of the station."

A woman is about to take her first airplane ride.
To the pilot, she says, "You will bring me back down, won't you?"
"Look lady, I've never left anybody up there yet."

And there's auto accident etiquette; who should speak first. And should a man precede a lady through the windshield.

"I've driven this car six years and never had a wreck."
"You mean you've driven this wreck six years and never had a car."

"Dad, I pulled your car around to the front door."
"Yeah, son, I hear it a knocking."

And there is family and personal:

"Just because I'm engaged to Joe doesn't mean I'm going to marry him."
"No dear. Of course not. He may back out."

"Hello."
"Hello, this is police lieutenant Smith. I think we've found you wife."
"What does she say?"
"Nothing."
"That's not my wife."

A mother and daughter from Georgia were visiting New York City. They hail a cab and as they're riding along the daughter asks the mother, "Who are all those ladies standing by lamp posts at corners?"
"They're waiting for their husbands to get off work."
The taxi driver says, "Why don't you tell her the truth, lady, they're prostitutes."
The daughter asks, "Mommy, do those ladies have children?"
The mother replies: "Of course they do. Where do you think Yankee cab drivers come from?"

"My husband tried to strike me and I want him arrested, officer."
"Where is he?"
"He's in intensive care."

"I look forward every Sunday to the afternoon nap."
"I thought you never took afternoon naps."
"I don't, but my wife does."

"I have no sympathy for a man who gets drunk every night."
"A man who gets drunk every night doesn't need sympathy."

"I hear Jones left everything he had to the orphan's home."
"Really, what did he have?"
"Twelve kids."

In those early digital papers there was a column by Ed Wynn that ran for several months. It was called, Ask Ed Wynn. Here is a question from a reader.

> Question: My friend has been acting strange ever since his wife ran off with a railroad engineer. Every time he hears a train whistle he runs and hides. What's wrong with him?
>
> Answer: It's only natural that he should react that way to a train whistle. He's afraid the engineer who stole his wife is bringing her back.

And then there's ethnic:

> "So, you are the defendant?"
> "No suh, judge. I'ze de one who stole de chickens."
>
> "Rastus, do the people across the road from you keep chickens?"
> "Day keeps some of dem, suh."
>
> "What are you men doing walking so slow up these stairs?"
> "We is working boss. We is carrying dis here desk up dese stairs."
> "I don't see any desk."
> "For lawd's sake, Rastus, we done forgot de desk."
>
> "Since I've drained the water from your ears young man they should clear up. You should be all right. How did you get water in your ears? Been swimming."
> "No, doctor. I'se been eating watermelon."

"Be steady Mrs. Johnson till you're fully immersed; be steady and you'll come up as white as snow."
"Oh, parson, dat's asking too much. A cream color will do."
"You say the defendant fired three shots at you in succession. Now, how far were you from him when he fired?"
"De fust one or de last one, suh?"
"Why, what difference does it make?"
"About a quarter of a mile, suh."

A little boy and his uncle from Canada were visiting New York City for the first time. The little boy had never seen a black person before. He pointed to a black woman, and said, "She's different, uncle."
"Yes, she's a colored lady."
"Is she that color all over?"
"She sure is."
"Gosh uncle, you know everything."

I found errors and retractions in those digital papers to be quite amusing. For example, this one appeared in September 1927. It reads: "It seems that in the write up of the Clemmons reunion September 4, an error was made as to a brother of Mr. Joe Clemmons being the father of 24 children. It seems that instead of it being a brother, it was an uncle or some near relative."

I'm glad the News-Record cleared that up.

The News-Record had a policy that items submitted had to be signed and have an address.

This is from June 22, 1928. "Mr. and Mrs. James Harrison have announced the engagement of their daughter, Ola, to Mr. Vernon Fox. The wedding date has not yet been fixed."

One week later this front page headline appeared with the following article: "News from California Creek, James Harrison's daughter is engaged to Vernon Fox was not true. The person who wrote in was a coward and signed a false name. It was sent in by some smart aleck who was ashamed to sign her name and signed a fictitious one."

Can't you just see James Harrison and his daughter walking into the News-Record office about the California Creek article? He says, "My daughter wouldn't be caught dead with that Fox boy."

Or, maybe it was the Fox boy who walks in, and says, "Why, that little yak, sputter, yammer, dit o' frack." Or, maybe there was no Vernon Fox. Who knows?

And speaking of foxes, here's another item that appeared in the May 11, 1928, issue, "Mrs. B.K. Davies and Mr. Paul Ellis went foxhunting last Saturday night."

I can envision a local wag on Spring Creek relating the following long winded tale:

> Paul Ellis and his friend walked into the News-Record office the Monday morning after the foxhunting article appeared in the paper. Banging on the counter, Ellis says, "I want to see the head zookeeper."
> A young man slouched behind the counter, asks, "Who?"
> Ellis says, "The head honcho, the big cheese, the one who slings ink at paper every week and calls it a weekly."
> "Oh, yes sir," says the young man, "I'll get Mr. Stamey."
> Mr. Stamey appears and says: "Hello, I'm H.G. Stamey, how can I help you?"
> "I'm Paul Ellis and last week you said me and Mrs. B.K. Davies went foxhunting. Let me ask you something. Does my

friend here," looking up at B.K., "who went foxhunting with me, look like Mrs. B.K. Davies? Not even with a skirt on. Calling him Mrs. B.K. Davies. Don't cry B.K."

"Let me check and see what happened."

The editor returns, and says: "It was sent in Mr. B.K. Davies. It looks like we made an error."

"You bet you did. You can't believe how upset my wife was. I woke up yesterday morning with egg on my face. I woke up this morning with I ain't saying what on my face. Ain't no fun sleeping in the chicken house.

"And B.K.'s wife is all tore up. She couldn't face the church folks, and her kids are all upset. Their little Tommy run away from home. Kids teasing the boy about his mother chasing foxes with a neighbor man. Don't cry B.K."

Editor Stamey says, "We'll run a retraction."

"That's good. It would be better if you come over to Meadows Store and explain it to the boys. They've been riding us high all weekend, wanting to know if while the dogs were running foxes, I was chasing B.K.'s wife. Don't cry B.K."

Editor Stamey ran this retraction the following week: "In Trust news last week an error appeared in type. One little 's' dropped in where it should not making it read, Mrs. B.K. Davies and Mr. Paul Ellis went foxhunting last Saturday night. That should have been Mr. B.K. Davies. Of course any reasonable reader would have known this was an error; but we regret that it occurred in the News-Record."

Jimmy Jack, you want to marry my daughter?
Okay, just remember, Mary Sue
has expensive tastes.

And speaking of hen houses, this one appeared in the early 30's. "Last year 32 billion eggs were consumed in the United States and 20 billion of them should have been consumed the year before."

Nothing like fresh eggs I always say.

The News-Record was a great paper in the late 20's and early 30's. Circulation was about 2,000 and many more county residents read it besides the subscribers. It had international news, national news, local news, farm news, religious news, and continuing novels. It was a good paper that required a lot of work to set that old type for a press that could break down at any time. You know, I think Adolph Hitler was a subscriber. The reason I say that is that some of those old ads are enclosed in swastikas.

Here is one last item from News-Record digital. Some of you would never forgive me if I didn't include this in humor heritage. This is from July 21, 1922. "Oldest Man, in World dies. Louisville, Kentucky. John Shell, 134 years old, reputed to be the oldest man in the world died at Creasy Creek near the city. Among his surviving children are 2 sons, one aged 90 years and one aged 7 years."

Can't you just see it:

> "Why don't you go out and play with me, pa, like other dads do?"
> "Look, son, I'm old and tired and don't bother me. Why don't you go outside and play and take your little seven-year-old kid brother with you."

I want to start with the original colonies and end at about 1965. I want to take a close look at our founding fathers, the minstrel show, traveling medicine show, the War for Southern Independence, Mark Twain, vaudeville, movies, radio, and beginning TV. Then we will narrow our focus to make it more local by looking at newspaper humor like Today's Chuckle, advice columns, and comics. We'll explore expressions, nicknames, and humor that I heard growing up to include some that I believe originated in this area. We will end with a semi-urban legend and the grapevine swing.

I want to briefly mention censorship. When I was growing up you could use the "n" word but not the "f" word. Now it has reversed. You can use the "f" word but not the "n" word.

So, what has changed in the past fifty years? I believe and tend to agree with a Nobel Prize winning economist Milton

Friedman who very well could have said, "The more socialistic a country becomes the less humor you tend to have." The Germans are the most socialistic country in the world. Read any translated German joke books lately?

Sure they're off color jokes. In today's atmosphere that's all that's left to joke about.

There has always been censorship. Fred Allen had a radio program in the thirties. One of the gags was, a girl married a husband that was so bad and abusive that she could have found a better one in a cemetery. It was stricken because it might hurt the feelings of cemetery owners. No Jewish jokes were permitted.

So much for censorship, now let us continue with facts, fiction and fantasy. There are some *f* words for you. And things do change. When I was growing up fantasy was spelled with a *ph*.

So, as Jackie Gleason would say on The Honeymooners, "And away we go."

Colonial Period

Jamestown was the first permanent settlement in North America. From 1609–1613, it was known as the "starving time." Hunger was so rampant that some resorted to cannibalism.

> A colonist meets a friend on a muddy Jamestown street, and he asks his friend, "Who did you have for dinner, Sunday?"
> "Just my mother-in-law," replies his friend. "I never realized until Sunday that she had such good taste."

What a way to start a country!

> In Philadelphia a young man asks a young lady, "Which way to your bedchamber?"
> "Through the church young man," replies the young lady, "through the church."

> As more colonists arrive, in Charleston a young man approaches a young lady with a pig under her arm. As he gets nearer the pig begins squealing violently.
> "My," says the young man, "your child is taking an awful fit."
> "It always does when it sees its daddy," she replies.

There was Manhattan Island that Dutchman Peter Minuit bought for twenty-four dollars in 1626. Isn't it amazing how values change? Today I wouldn't give you a dime for Manhattan Island.

Ugh! We keep um land or pale face blow um smoke.

Notice there were no jokes in the northern colonies. Puritans didn't laugh much, but they did smile once in a while. That's when they saw a witch hanging from a tree. The higher up in the tree the broader the smile.

New England puritans were a hard working industrious lot. They were into manufacturing and shipping. They had some of the best equipped slave ships on the high seas. At home they had high strung wives who couldn't wait to free the slaves once they were settled on a southern plantation. Most of our ancestors came through South Carolina and Virginia. They passed by plantations that were called Tuckahoe.

As one of my early ancestors was passing, I can hear a plantation owner say, "Want to share crop some cotton, Mac?"

"No thanks, Tuckahoe," replies my ancestor, "we'll just cross the mountain and find our own land."

Slaves and back woodsmen are a part of our humor heritage. Slavery tends to work in isolated settings but not where people are in close proximity to one another. Interactions in the city tend to destroy that institution.

From 1687–1741 there was a slave revolt on the average of every two and one half years in New York City. In 1712, a revolt left nine whites dead and twenty-one slaves were executed. In 1726, a privy was set on fire. When locals tried to fight it, they were set upon by a mob and several were killed. History doesn't record whether or not anyone was in the privy at the time the fire was set. Sometimes I wonder about historians.

In 1741, a series of fires broke out in New York City. In that year New York City had a population of one-hundred-thousand and twenty percent of them were slaves. The city was on edge because the slaves threatened to kill all the white men, take the white women, and elect a king. Hey, that's right out of the Mel Brooks' movie, *Blazing Saddles*: "Where de white women at?"

A reward was offered to find out who was behind the fires. This is how the offer went, and you can't make this stuff up; one-hundred pounds for white testimony, forty pounds for free black testimony, and twenty pounds and freedom for black slave testimony. It worked because a one-hundred pound reward was paid. As a result thirteen blacks and four whites were hanged, thirteen blacks were burned at the stake, and one-hundred people were banished from the city.

Founding Fathers

In a day when we are losing sight of our founding, I would like to revisit our early heritage. From the Indian Wars George Washington returned wearing his British army uniform. He was sitting in a Williamsburg tavern and was talking with Henry Lee, I believe it was. Their conversation probably went something like this:

> "Henry, I'm getting out of the army," says George. "The British only promote their own."
>
> "I don't blame you George," replies Henry. "You ought to quit pining for that Fairfax gal and think about settling down and taking a wife. Heck, Sally is a married woman for crying out loud."
>
> "I don't know, Henry. I'm getting some age on me, my teeth are falling out, and I have these pockmarks from smallpox."
>
> "Nonsense, George, you're only twenty-six and there's Martha."
>
> "Martha who?"
>
> "Martha Dandridge."
>
> "That homely little flirt."

"George, she married, Dan Custis, and he dropped deader than four o'clock. That homely little flirt inherited a fortune, seventeen-thousand-five-hundred acres of land, and three-hundred slaves."

"Hmm. A fortune, seventeen-thousand-five-hundred acres, and three-hundred slaves. Thinking back, she was cuter than a speckled pup. I'll have to drop in; and see her."

"I wouldn't wait too long, George. That rich Charles Carter wants her hand."

"I'll see her this very day. By the way, Dan's old man, John Custis IV, wouldn't let him dream of marrying. He threatened to cut Dan off without a shilling if he took a wife. Of course, John was dead set against marriage because he and his wife were in a constant battle. I think old John spent too much time down at his slave quarters, if you get my drift. How did Martha get Dan to marry her?"

"Old man John Custis IV was against Martha, too. Know what I think, George? I think she bewitched the old man."

"Bewitched him?"

"Yeah, According to the white house pickannies at the Custis place, that little eighteen-year-old Martha took thirty-nine-year-old Dan by the hand, marched right into the Custis mansion, and slammed the door behind herself and Dan. She took the old man's face in her hands, and began to sing something like this: 'John Custis I-Vee, your son Dan is the man for me, because I'm a lady, I'm a female lady, l-a-d-y, female la—,' Where are you going George?"

> "Every eye in the joint is on us. You've embarrassed the devil out of me. I'd rather be dodging Indian arrows and tomahawks than be seen putting up with your singing."

At the time of the Revolutionary War, the New England colonies were the most prepared to break away from England. They had a network of correspondence with the other colonies and had what they called "Minutemen" that would ride horses through the countryside to warn of approaching British troops. New England was well organized and the most prepared to revolt.

One such horseman was Paul Revere. One day he was riding through the countryside shouting:

> "The British are coming! The British are coming! To arms, the British are coming!"
> A pretty young colonist sticks her head out an upstairs window, and replies, "I can't; my husband is in the Caribbean."
> A quick thinking Paul Revere says, "Whoa!"

At the Constitutional convention there were five on the committee selected to write the Declaration of Independence. Committee chairman John Adams had written one previously and most of the middle colony delegates walked out. Adams once essentially said that the colonies were not going to be England's "door mat."

John had a bull-whip for a tongue. He's the one who said that Alexander Hamilton was the bastard brat of a Scottish peddler. I think John graduated from an Attila the Hun charm school.

> Adams says, "Who wants to write this thing?"
> Robert Livingston and Roger Sherman, each said, "I don't"
> "I don't either," says Ben Franklin, "I don't like corrections being made to my work."
> "I don't either. It's hot, and I'm not used to this climate," replies John Adams. "Besides, I wrote one back of this and the middle colony delegates walked out."
> Ben Franklin looked over at Thomas Jefferson, and he says, "Let's let Tuckahoe Tom write it." Tuckahoe was the name of Jefferson's boyhood home.

After independence was declared George Washington, in his military uniform, went to get a flag made. At that time there were several ladies in Philadelphia who could have sewn it. One would have been seamstress Rebecca Flower Young who stitched a Union Jack where the stars are now located on Old Glory. Another candidate was Betsy Griscom Ross who ran an upholstery business. Which one would Washington choose?

Well, let's look at the facts. In 1776 Rebecca Young was thirty-six-year-old, has six children, and was nursing her sixth child. Betsy Ross was a good looking twenty-four old childless widow. Maybe George was enamel challenged, but he wasn't blind.

There's a story of George Washington and James Madison walking down a Philadelphia street. In my history book sixty years ago, George was said to be six feet tall. Today, sources tell us that George was six feet two inches tall. If George keeps growing in three-hundred years he'll be seven feet tall.

> Anyway, they're walking down High Street in Philadelphia and from behind, a voice says, "Hey shorty."
> They keep walking. James Madison is four feet eleven inches tall and weighs ninety-five pounds. From behind the voice yells louder, "Hey shorty!"
> James reaches up and tugs the sleeve of George's army uniform, and George looks down.
> Looking up at George, James says, "George, I think somebody is calling you."

Let me go back to that child in Rebecca Young's arms in 1776. Fast forward to 1813, she is Mary Young Pickersgill and living in Baltimore, Maryland. She is approached by George Armistead and John Stricker from Fort McHenry about making a storm flag, and also, a flag with the stars and stripes.

> George asks, "Can you make us a stars and stripes flag thirty by forty-two?"
> "Sure," says Mary. "My mother made flags all the time."
> "That's thirty feet by forty-two feet," George adds.
> Mary says, "Oh!"

She agreed to make the flags. It took five weeks and four-hundred yards of material. These flags were so large that it took the whole family, extended family, and half the neighborhood to stitch them. To gain space they leased Claggett's Brewery at night. While the women were stitching the flags, historians don't tell how they kept the men folk out of the brew. That Old Glory flag cost $406.90, and it took eleven men to hoist it up the flagpole.

The flag was passed down through the Armistead family, and it came to rest in the Smithsonian. In 1998 they did a conservation treatment of this "Star Spangled Banner Flag" at a cost of eighteen-million dollars.

Our senior founding father was Benjamin Franklin. He escaped his brother's Boston printing business and at seventeen was in Philadelphia where he wanted to marry fifteen-year-old Deborah Read. Ben didn't have two nickels to rub together. That's because back then currency was in pounds, pence, and pennies.

So, in 1723 the mother marries Deborah off to John Rogers and gives him a dowry. He absconds to the Caribbean, leaves them with a mountain of bills, and is never seen or heard from again. Seven years later in 1730, Ben returns from England with his son, William, and they set up housekeeping with Deborah. Historians are polite and call theirs a common law marriage. When I was growing up, we had another name for it. Oh, never mind.

Ben would have made a great stand-up comic. Here are some lines he probably ran by Deborah:

> We are all born ignorant. We must work hard to remain stupid.
>
> Some people die at twenty-five and are not buried until they are seventy-five

> Any fool can criticize, condemn, and complain: and most fools do.

> He that is good at excuses is seldom good for anything else.

I wake up every morning and grab the morning paper. Then I look at the obituary page. If my name's not on it, I get up.

That reminds me. A lot of people in our area have the same name. I saw mine in the Asheville Citizen on the obituary page one day, and I called a friend, and asked: "Hey Joe, did you see the morning paper today? My name is on the obituary page."

"No. Where are you calling from?" he replies.

Let's get back to Ben. Guests, like fish, begin to smell after three days.

> Three can keep a secret if two of them are dead.
>
> He that lives on hope will die fasting.
>
> A man between two lawyers is like a fish between two cats.
>
> If you want to know the value of money, go try to borrow some.
>
> The art of acting is keeping people from coughing.

In wine there is wisdom, in beer there is freedom, in water there is bacteria. You know, W.C. Fields couldn't have said it better.

The problem with doing nothing is not knowing when you are finished.

Name it Washington! What do you fellows have against me?

Blessed is he who expects nothing for he will never be disappointed.

Old boys have their playthings as well as young ones; their difference is only in the price. I think this is what Ben meant to say, "The only difference between men and boys is the price of their toys."

God heals, the doctor collects the fees.

Originality is the art of concealing your sources.

> Beware of the young doctor and the old barber.
>
> Politicians are like diapers. They should be changed often and for the same reasons.
>
> I'd rather be a pessimist because I can only be pleasantly surprised.

"Like those Deb? Try these."

> To find a girl's faults praise her to her girl friends.
>
> He that displays too often his wife and wallet is in danger of having both of them borrowed.
>
> Keep both eyes open before marriage and half shut afterward.
>
> Never take a wife until you have a house and a fire to put her in.
>
> When man and woman die, as poets sung, his heart the last part moves, her last, the tongue.

"How do you like those last ones, Deb?"
"You know how to get me started don't you, Ben? Why don't you take your jug, your 'B' Bill, and go fly a kite?" Wonder what she meant by the B?

When George Washington married Martha Dandridge Custis, she owned twenty-seven square miles of land spread across five

Virginia counties. George bought land as a surveyor, inherited Mt. Vernon, and was coming into thirty-one square miles of land awarded to him for his soldering during the Indian Wars. It was difficult for historians to determine if theirs was a marriage or a merger.

Dean Martin says that the reason George was standing in that boat crossing the Delaware was that someone thought they saw Dolly Madison skinny dipping. Hey, Dean! (Looking at the ceiling, then down at the floor.) I'm not thinking he's down there, he always said he spread across more floors than Johnson's Wax. In 1776 Dolly would have been Dolly Payne, and she would have been eight years old. Not only that, there was supposedly enough ice chunks in the river that evening to mix Dean's drinks for three days.

George Washington's mother, Mary Ball Washington, was a dyed in the wool British loyalist. When George visited her during the revolution, she would ask, "Well, George, how many battles did you lose this week?" And when Benedict Arnold deserted to the British side, she said, "Well, George, looks like you lost the only smart general you had." George must have been a saint.

Alexander Hamilton, the one John Adams called the bastard brat of a Scottish peddler, was born in the Caribbean to Rachel Faucette. She was married to John Michael Levine, took up with James Hamilton, and some historians assert that Alexander's father was Thomas Stevens. Evidently, there wasn't a man in the Caribbean that couldn't turn Faucette on.

Alexander went from pillar to post growing up, but he was brilliant. At fifteen when the owner took sick, he ran an export and import business where he was working. He was writing brilliant letters to a local newspaper, and some of the folks decided to send him to King College in New York City. As Washington was making his retreat from New York City, he spotted Hamilton leading a group of cadets preparing defenses. He was so impressed by his leadership that he immediately put him on his staff. Hamilton became Washington's most trusted aide.

In 1791 Hamilton is married to Elizabeth Schuyler and they have a family. While Secretary of the Treasury, thirty-seven-year-old Hamilton is accosted by twenty-three-year-old Maria Lewis Reynolds on a Philadelphia street. She relates a sob story that she is destitute and needs four-hundred dollars to get to New York City. Hamilton goes to the bank, draws out the money, and takes the money up to her room. It must have been in gold bars because he kept going up to her room for the next three years. Gold's pretty heavy stuff, you know, and hard to carry. Not only that, back then it took a lot of planning to make a trip from Philadelphia to New York. I dare say this trip from Philadelphia to New York was the most thoroughly planned scenic trip in American history. After three years Hamilton is out several thousand dollars.

Husband, James Reynolds, who sanctioned the affair, is caught counterfeiting. To get out of the jam he threatens Hamilton with blackmail. Hamilton, like Paul Revere, says, "Whoa, I want no part of this." So, Reynolds goes to Hamilton's enemies. James Monroe and Aaron Burr interview Hamilton and are satisfied that no treasury money is stolen. Rumors keep flying that treasury money is being used to finance this affair, and James Monroe and Congressman Frederick Muhlenberg interview Hamilton again. With the promise that they will be kept secret, Hamilton, to prove his innocence, hands over to Monroe the love letters written to him by Maria Reynolds. They verify that no treasury money was stolen. This is in 1794.

Let us fast forward to 1797. James Thomson Callender prints these Reynolds love letters in a pamphlet and distributes them throughout the new states that were recently colonies. Hamilton is furious and confronts Monroe and challenges him to a duel. Aaron Burr intercedes. He says, "Look fellows, what do you think this is, the Wild West?"

To rebut the publication of his love letters from Maria, Hamilton wrote his own pamphlet. In it he confesses to having the affair, and apologizes because he felt that his honor was being impugned. In effect, the pamphlet said, "I didn't steal a dime from the Treasury. I was merely a married man having an affair with a consenting married woman."

I'm reminded of an East Tennessee story. An old farmer and a friend are sitting on the farmer's front porch when, with a rooster under his arm, his son walks down the path toward them.

> The farmer asks, "Where did you get the rooster, boy?"
> "Stole him, pa."
> The old farmer turns to his friend, slaps him on the back, and says: "That's my boy. He may steal, but he won't lie."

How did these Reynolds love letters get into print? Well, Monroe gave the letters to Thomas Jefferson who paid James Callender to publish them. Later, and for a fee, Callender published a pamphlet making the charge that Jefferson had children by his slave Sally Hemings. No, I don't think Jefferson paid Callender to publish those Hemings accusations.

Ah, those founding days; had Charles Dickens been alive at the time, he might have said, "It was the best of times and it was the worst of times."

What did Hamilton's wife, Elizabeth, think about this scandal? According to historians their marriage became stronger than ever. What in the world did he tell her? Here we have some valuable information that half the married men in America could use, and historians don't tell us. I mean, just when they could really be of benefit, they draw a blank and come up empty. What's the deal with historians?

Sometimes I wonder about Hamilton. Here's a man who can talk his wife into forgetting about his illicit affair with a married woman, and he can't talk his way out of a gunfight. Makes me think he could handle a woman better than he could a pistol.

Speaking of duels; Andrew Jackson was six feet two inches tall and weighed one-hundred-forty-nine pounds. A strong puff of wind would blow him sideways. He had a duel every so often to pick up enough lead to keep him weighed down. Most of his duels were over his marriage to Rachel and her questionable divorce from Lewis Robards. Why didn't Andy check with Ben Franklin?

I'm reminded of a Marx brother gag in *Duck Soup*, not that Rachel was that kind of woman. With bullets and shells flying in a war scene, Groucho says, "Remember men, we're fighting for this woman's honor, which is probably more than she ever did."

To me, the funniest part of the Marx joke was that leading lady, Margaret Dumont, didn't catch the humor.

What Jackson did for the country at New Orleans was nothing short of a miracle. After that battle, Americans said, "Look at what we can do." Now, we could fight among ourselves with pride.

While we're on duels, nobody challenged John Adams to a duel. He would have beaten an opponent to death with his tongue before they reached the dueling ground. Somebody else who was never challenged to a duel was James Madison. At four feet eleven and weighing ninety-five pounds, he could have turned sideways and all his opponent would have seen was Madison's dueling pistol.

I don't know if Madison could shoot Straight or not but there was nothing wrong with his eyesight. That Dolly Payne Todd, wow! Black hair, blue eyes, rosy complexion, and a knock out figure; she caused Ben Franklin's bifocals to fog up, and he forgot them in France. An intellectual in Philadelphia was a man who could describe Dolly without throwing his arms out of socket.

As Vice President, John Adams wanted the President to be addressed as "His Highness," or "His Lordship the President of the United States." In the Senate it earned him the nickname of "His Rotundity." It was the Senate's polite way of saying "His Lard Bucket." I suppose a Puritan can be funny.

President John Adams signed the Alien Sedition Acts. The alien part basically said that if you were in the country for less than five years and caused trouble, you could be deported. The sedition part allowed critics of the government, meaning the press, to be fined and imprisoned. Under the sedition part of the act, several editors were prosecuted and sent to jail. One victim of this law was Ben Franklin's grandson, Benjamin Franklin Bache. The federalist press called him "lightning rod, Jr." Now that's funny even if it did come from the federalist press. Sometimes you wonder why we broke away from the Crown if our government was going to be worse.

Life is so unfair. There's George Washington with false teeth, and it should have been John Adams. He had a wrecking ball on his tongue that would knock anybody's teeth out, excluding his own.

There was John's wife, Abigail. I don't know whether she wanted to be the President's wife or a Carrie Nation role model. Just kidding! I'm just kidding. It must have been tough for Abigail trying to keep the home fires burning with the kids while John was out all the time…insulting folks.

Let's briefly look at Carry Nation.

> One day Carry came home all tired and tuckered out from busting up a saloon. "Why," her husband asks, "don't you take a hatchet next time so you can really do some damage?"
> "You know Dave," replies Carrie, "that's the most sensible thing you've said since we tied the knot."

Thomas Jefferson was the first President to move into the white House in Washington. Upon seeing it for the first time, he said it was big enough for two emperors, a pope, and an Arab sheik. Historians don't tell us if the sheik came with or without his harem.

One day Robert Livingston rushes into the White House, and says, "Mr. President, we can by the Louisiana Territory for less than two cents and acre. It's unconstitutional, what should we do?"

"Buy it," replies President Jefferson, "it's cheaper than stealing it."

In 1794 James Madison was forty-three years old. He married the gorgeous twenty-six-year-old widow, Dolly Payne Todd, who was five feet six and one half inches tall. Oh, I would have loved to have seen Dolly in the early 1790's. When she walked down the streets of Philadelphia, men stopped and stared. They even knew what time she took her daily stroll and made a point to be on the street to see her. Men would wave, and I don't know if they made wolf whistles back then or not; but, wow! Dolly was one good looking lady.

Please marry me, Dolly.
I'll always look up to you.

Federalist papers said James needed to climb a ladder to kiss Dolly. In 1794 I would have climbed Mt. Everest to have kissed her. One sad page in American history, Dolly Madison never got to meet me. Hope my wife doesn't kill me before I get home tonight. Hugh, Joe, or Dan, would one of you fellows call my house later tonight to see if I made it? Oh, you're an understanding audience.

Imagine this scene: In 1794 James Madison and Dolly Payne Todd are dating and they walk up to the door at 190 High Street in Philadelphia. A servant answers the door. From the foyer she and James see seated in the living room Vice President John Adams and his wife Abigail, Secretary of the Treasury Alexander Hamilton and his wife Elizabeth, Secretary of War Henry Knox and his wife Lucy, Attorney General William Bradford and his wife Susan, House speaker Frederick Muhlenberg and his wife Catherine, and Robert Morris who is married to a White woman. That's right, Mary White. Seated across from them is Martha Washington. As they are standing there, George Washington, wearing his army uniform, enters from another room and joins Martha.

While looking at this distinguished group of America's leadership, Dolly's mouth falls open in awe. Wow!

And the men staring at Dolly, their mouths fall open in awe. Wow!

> Introductions are made and the men and women retire to separate parlors. In the Men's parlor, Robert Morris says, "I've got a ladder you can borrow, James, if you want to kiss Dolly."
> "If Dolly doesn't love you," adds Frederick Muhlenberg, "tell her you'll grow on her."

"James," says John Adams, "if you grew on her, you still wouldn't be bigger than a birthmark."

"Okay men, knock it off. You're setting a bad precedent," says George Washington.

I want to briefly mention Robert Morris. He was born in 1732 in Liverpool, England, and was George Washington's close friend. He was one of two men who signed the Declaration of Independence, the Articles of Confederation, and the United States Constitution. I think he had writer's cramp from signing all those historical documents.

For one dollar a year, he leased this house at 190 High Street to the city of Philadelphia for the President's residence. Morris made a fortune in banking and shipping and would be what we today would call a tycoon. During the Revolution, Morris was in charge of the colonial navy and personally owned two-hundred and fifty ships. His fleet kept Washington informed of British troop movements and guided the French navy into Yorktown where the war ended. While the colonies provided $800,000 toward the war effort, Morris chipped in $74,000,000 from his personal fortune that he did not expect to be repaid. It was his $10,000 which kept the soldiers together for the battle of Princeton. It was Morris script that kept Washington's officers from mutinying at the end of the war.

In 1780 when Pennsylvania went bankrupt, Morris was selected to fix it. He solved their financial problems by opening Pennsylvania ports to commerce and by allowing the free market to set prices. During the war he set up a banking system for the independent colonies and introduced the decimal system with a dollar sign for our currency. Also, he wrote a booklet "On Public Credit" which was Alexander Hamilton's blueprint for a national bank. While Adam Smith was writing Wealth of Nations, Robert Morris was practicing it. Back when history was taught, historians, in my opinion, ignored Morris.

> In the ladies parlor, Martha says, "I understand you're engaged to Mr. Madison, Dolly."
> Dolly says, "Oh, I don't know."
> Martha replies: "Oh Dolly, be proud. James will make you a fine husband."
> What was Dolly supposed to say, "I'll marry him when he grows up?"
> Elizabeth Hamilton asks, "Is it true Martha, that your husband threw a silver dollar across the Potomac?"
> "I don't know how these things get started," replies Martha. "There is a place in western Virginia where I threw George across the Potomac."
>
> Mary Morris asks, "Is it true about George sleeping in all those beds?"
> "I'd say that it is," answers Martha, "but George couldn't do any damage. Nobody can get him out of his army uniform."

Dolly had a son by her first husband, John Todd, a Philadelphia lawyer. She called the child Payne, P-A-Y-N-E, and he was a pain, p-a-i-n. Oh, what a brat he must have been. This reminds me of the story of a farmer who married a beautiful widow that had a bratty ten-year-old son.

> She goes shopping for some things to fancy up the old farm house. She returns from shopping, and asks her son, "How did you get along with your new daddy?"
> "Oh, it was wonderful mom. He took me out on the lake twice and I swam back to shore."
> "That's a pretty long swim, son."
> "It wasn't so bad, mom, once I got out of the tow sack."

I've often wondered why James didn't discipline the kid. But, I guess it was because the kid was bigger than he was. Dolly would walk down a Washington street with James and Payne, and folks would say, "There goes Dolly and her two boys."

> One day James asked Payne, "What comes after ten?"
> "Jack," replies Payne.

When Payne was twenty-three, James sent him to Paris with the delegation to sign the treaty to end the War of 1812. He thought it would be educational and it was. Payne didn't attend any of the treaty meetings, but he was in and out of every gambling house in Paris and the rest of Europe.

Dolly Madison was famous for her social graces and tact. She instinctively knew how to treat people to make them feel important. The amazing thing to me was that she did it without attending an institution of higher learning. Everyone loved to socialize with Dolly.

Once I mentioned to my Uncle Max, Dolly's role in history. I explained that at that time the White House was the only place in Washington large enough to host big parties and social gatherings. For Sixteen years Dolly was hostess for Thomas Jefferson and her husband, James. Her dinners and parties were attended by important people in Washington, and a few guests had some rough edges which reflected a rugged frontier mentality. In the course of an evening, a few would become rowdy and difficult to control. Dolly had the charm, grace, and tact to exert a calming influence on the most crude and abusive guest. For this, attendees loved, admired, and respected her.

Know what my Uncle Max said? He said: "Boy, that woman had a gift. She knew how to handle drunks."

After she married James she began to wear large turban hats. That was so that when she and James were traveling and James got tired, he could curl up inside the hat. It was sort of like a sleeping bag. One day she forgot that he was in it and had him on her head before he fell out. He was almost killed in the fall.

I've kidded about James Madison. From the chin down he was a midget, but from the chin up, he was a giant. He fathered a Constitution and the Bill of Rights for four million people who were in the country at that time. Heck, today we have four million people who are trying to shred these documents, and that's just the government workers.

I'm amazed at the number of founding fathers who were poor public speakers. There was Thomas Jefferson who spoke barely above a whisper, James Madison who couldn't be heard beyond the third row in a church sanctuary, and Alexander Hamilton who didn't have to speak because he could write so well. Another founding father who didn't have to speak well was Robert Morris because he was behind the scenes providing the financial wizardry for the break with England. George Washington wasn't a good speaker, but I understand, was gifted at cursing. I guess the reason that razor tongued John Adams went so far in early politics was because he was a heavy set, loud mouthed lawyer. With his precedent, we've been filling elective offices with loud mouthed lawyers ever since.

Please allow me to add one final note about our founding fathers. It seems to me that with the exception of Ben Franklin, they were the only group of leaders in history who were statesmen before they became politicians.

The Minstrel Show

The Minstrel show was a northern enterprise that began around 1820. It was a parody of life on the southern plantation as viewed by northern entertainment enterprises that financed actors, skits, and shows. This new form of public amusement was created for northern audiences because that's where the money, venues, and actors were.

The minstrel show was a variety show that featured singing, dancing, humor, and other acts. It usually started with a march of white actors in blackface strutting on stage. This cakewalk, as they called it, was mocking the white plantation owner's walk. They arranged themselves in a semicircle with the leader or interlocutor in the middle. The end men usually featured one short fat man and a tall skinny one that cracked jokes between one another.

>For instance, one shouts across the stage to the other, and says, "There was a fire in a clock shop uptown, today."
>"Any damage?" replies the other.
>"No," replies the first, "just lots of second hand smoke."

>"What chew doing now, Rastus?"
>"I'se an exporter."
>"An exporter?"
>"Yeah, I'se got fired from de Pullman Company."

The minstrel show reached its peak in the 1840's. In 1837 Thomas Dartmouth "Daddy" Rice, who was born in Brooklyn, New York, picked up the "Jim Crow" song and dance from a stable hand in Louisville, Kentucky. He was so impressed that he even bought the tattered clothing the man was wearing. How the stable-hand got home without his clothing, I don't know. Maybe he sneaked home after dark. There would have been less chance of him being spotted.

Rice added verses and continued to perfect the song for years. This is the original "Jim Crow" song. Remember, Daddy Rice is in blackface and singing to the music while dancing.

JIM CROW

Come listen all you gals and boys
I's jist from Tuckyhoe.
I'm goin to sing a little song,
My name is Jim Crow.

Fist on de heel tap,
Den on the toe
Ebry time I wheel about
I jump Jim Crow.

Weel about and turn about
En do jus so.
And every time I wheel about
I jump Jim Crow.

Tuckahoe is an Indian word for an edible moss. It came to mean any slave holding plantation in Virginia or the Carolinas.

With this song Rice's minstrel show became a huge hit. Audiences all over the country clamored to get a ticket to see Rice perform, and he became an over night sensation like the country had never seen before. Daddy Rice became wealthy and this piece of new culture captivated northern white audiences. In fact, thanks to the "Jim Crow" song, the minstrel show became popular in Europe. This song became the first international hit.

A staple of the minstrel show was the stump speech. It was a speech usually given by a big, heavy set, white man in blackface who acted self important while he mangled the words. Here is an example of a stump-speech:

> Thank youse folks for allowing me to speak here today on dis suspicious occasion. Thank youse for dat fine introduction mister interlocutor. I'se wants to thank all youse folks who dissembled here today for de opportunity to speak.
>
> It's not every day dat I'se gets to speak to such a fine, outstanding august group like dis. Or September group, or October group, but never de less, I'se proud to be here to speaks to you today. I'se thankful to live in a country where a man like me can run fer office. I'se wants youse to know I'se for freedoms and libertines.
>
> Since dis here campaign began, I'se been accused of spending time kissing babies. I'se want youse to know dat I'se hates kissing babies. It's de mamas I'se wants to be kissing.

My opponent in dis here campaign says dat I'se ain't fit to be a dogcatcher. Well folks, I'se ain't running fer no dogcatcher. I'se want's to be day mayor, and I'se wants to be your night mayor too.

Now, some of duh folks in dis here town is for decoloration of de water supply, and some folks in dis here town is agin decoloration of de water supply. I'se wants youse to know right now that I'se gonna stan by duh folks.

We have a town treasurer who is tall and short. He's six feet five inches tall, and our treasury is two-million-three-hundred-thousand dollars short.

Folks done ax me what I'se going to do about the liquor and da beer. I'se wants youse to know, I'se going to take care o' duh liquor and duh beer (patting stomach).

And day ax what I'se going to do about illegal gambling. Well, I'se gonna formulate a plan to take care duh problem. And I'll lay three to one odds that I'se comes up wid a plan fore my term is ober. You can bet your last dollar I'se going to fix de problem.

Now, I'se been asked about duh girls a hanging around duh lamp posts under de gas lights on Dove Street. Women trying to entice our fine young men to go astray. I'se tell youse what I'se gonna do. I'se going down dare personally to check it out fer myself to see if duh boys are gittin day money's worth. Dat's what I aims to do.

As your mayor I'se going to cut taxes and build a fine new city hall, pave all duh roads, and put in sidewalks all across duh city. And I'se ain't gonna hire none o' my friends into big high paying city jobs. Dats reserved for duh family, in-laws, and kinfolk.

Yes sir. Votes fer me fore yore mayor and wese ken works together to make dis a town dat wese can be proud of.

Stephen Foster wrote songs for the minstrel show. It must have been quite a colorful spectacle with all the costumes, music, dancing, and the blackface. Can't you just see them on stage singing "Camptown Races," or "Oh, Susannah" while a half dozen musicians are strumming their banjos. The only time Stephen Foster ever went south was when he took his wife to New Orleans on their honeymoon. Harriet Beecher Stowe reportedly got her distorted view of plantation life from attending minstrel shows.

Why, you're Stephen Foster. This buggy is a cream puff. You can have it for a song.

It seems that everything in genealogy goes back to the War for Southern Independence. Here is one example of Lincoln's humor and two others from that era:

> A bureaucrat died and an office seeker rushes in to see Lincoln to ask if he could take his place.
> "It's all right with me," replies Lincoln, "if it's all right with the undertaker."

> A soldier told his girlfriend that he would write her every day. He wrote her every day for seven months, and one day he got a letter saying that she was marrying somebody else. He wrote his family to find out who it was. They wrote back that it was her letter carrier.

David Buskirk of the 27th Indiana regiment was seven feet tall and weighed three-hundred-eighty pounds. He was captured in 1862 and sent to a Richmond prison. Since, in those days, a seven footer was a novelty, Jeff Davis went to see him. Buskirk told Davis that his six sisters saw him off on the train.

Last Friday morning, Mr. and Mrs. Mark Banks saw Mrs. Banks' mother, that was visiting them, off on a Southern Railway passenger train.

He said, "As I was standing there ready to board, they all came up to me and each of them leaned down and kissed the top of my head."

It seems that more jokes were recorded in the north. You know how that goes; the winner writes the joke books.

I think the south cemented some of their humor in a song. It's hard to be humorous in a song but if you read "Goober Peas," I think that you will agree that the writer did about as well as can be done with humor in a song. I believe the second verse sums it up best.

Goober Peas

> Just before the battle the general hears a row
> He says, "The Yanks are coming, I hear their rifles now."
> He turns around in wonder, and what d'ya think the sees?
> It's the Georgia militia eating goober peas.

A "case of Yankee chills" is the Confederate definition of a coward.

The traveling medicine show had its roots in Europe. In the course of time, it found its way to the colonies and like so many institutions; it developed new wrinkles and changed over time. In America a few days before the wagon arrived in an area, handbills were passed out in the town where the show was to perform. The main idea was to attract a crowd with amusements and sell bottles of liquid patent medicine that were blended with concoctions of opium, cocaine, and other ingredients mixed with alcohol. To draw an audience there were singers, acrobatic acts, ventriloquists, flea circuses, story tellers, and any sort of entertainment that would pique a person's curiosity. Plenty of snake oil was sold in this fashion.

Later, in the 1880's big pharmacy saw the value in the medicine show. These companies hired mountebanks that traveled by wagon all across America to hawk their patent medicines. The medicine show was regulated out of business, more or less, by federal laws passed in the 1930's. Hadacol was the last of the medicine shows. It ended in the early 1950's.

Other forms of entertainment during the period after the War for Southern Independence were the circus and the Wild West Show.

Vaudeville Forward

Before we get started, I received a couple of notes about my July presentation. The first one says: "Dear A.E., You mentioned writing about your humor heritage in your second childhood. You are technically incorrect. You shouldn't be talking about your second childhood because you are not through your first childhood yet. Your loving wife, G.R.P."

Okay, here's another one.

> "Dear A.E.,
> I heard you are now doing comedy and folks are hanging on your every word. That must be quite a shock for you. When you were in politics and running for office, nobody cared what you said.
> Sincerely,
> Chairman K.B. Fish."

Let me do a quick review of the first presentation. In the first part we examined our humor heritage by looking at News-Record Digital, our beginning colonies, our founding fathers, the minstrel show, the traveling medicine show, and the War for Southern Independence. We reviewed some of the humor used as fillers in those old News-Records that included mechanical, family, and ethic.

Mechanical: A lady withdrew her petition for divorce and bought her husband an airplane. She figured hiring an undertaker would be cheaper than paying a lawyer.

Family: A neighbor lady was sick and the mother to her small daughter, says, "Susie, run across the road and see how old lady Parker is." The child returns in a few minutes, and says, "Mrs. Parker says it's none of your business how old she is."

Ethnic: The judge says, "Rastus, I don't want to see you in my court again."
"Why judge, youse going to retire."

In colonial times there was very little written humor although I'm sure that our Irish and Scottish ancestors had a good sense of humor. For instance, a Scotchman chases a rolling silver dollar into the roadway and is run over and killed by a team of runaway horses. The authorities ruled his death to be by natural causes.

I'm inclined to believe that New England Puritans frowned on laughter. It's really a shame that New England, in my humble opinion, wasn't named either Upper Transylvania or New Dracula.

We looked at some of our founding fathers. I think we decided that John Adams attended an Attila the Hun charm school. Ben Franklin was a giant with intellect, organizational skills, inventions, diplomacy, and humor. Robert Morris, though hardly mentioned in our history books, financed a larger part of the revolution with the money he earned from his banking and mercantile investments. George Washington, with his tenacity and bravery, provided the grunt work to the ideal of breaking away from the Mother Country and let his protégé, Alexander Hamilton, follow the Robert Morris blueprint for a national banking system. And, of course, there was Thomas Jefferson who put into words the intent of the revolt by writing the Declaration of Independence. The founders provided us with one of the few governments in mankind's history that did not feature a tyrant subduing the masses and making them subservient to his whim. We escaped the curse of dictators thanks to our founders.

I picked on James Madison because he was short. He not only fathered the Constitution and Bill of Rights and influenced the individual colonies to approve them, but he and Dolly breathed life into the institutions created by the new Constitution. Thomas Jefferson gets most of the credit for the founding by writing the Declaration, but most revolutions bog down into chaos and internal strife. Revolutions, as a rule, leave those revolting in worse condition than before.

James Madison's writing provided a blueprint for a new form of government. Not only did the Constitution provide the framework for government, but he and Dolly gave it legs and nurtured the fledgling republic until these new institutions were established and accepted. At the time of the founding our country's most brilliant minds, without adequate compensation, were dedicated to public service. Today, our most brilliant minds have discovered that the government is where the compensation is. You know, like hungry hogs running to slop.

We looked at the minstrel show that featured white performers in blackface. These were northern enterprises using northern actors, facilities, and money because that's where the population was located. The minstrel show was the rage, thanks in part to Daddy Rice and the infusion of a new culture into a Caucasian population. A group called Christy Minstrels sang the songs written by Stephen Foster for their stage production. Abe Lincoln loved the song of the century "Dixie" so much that he had it played at his political rallies and again after Lee surrendered at Appomattox. "Dixie" came from a minstrel show.

Now, let me continue with facts, fiction, and fantasy.

But, before I do, I want to mention briefly that in 1832 just about every building in Fayetteville, N.C., burned to the ground. So, in Raleigh, Governor Montford Stokes hired contractor Thomas Bragg to fireproof the state capitol building. Wouldn't you know that just as the workmen were applying the finishing touches on fireproofing the capitol building, it burned to the ground? As Governor Stokes and contractor Bragg were sifting through the ashes a few days later, the governor picks up a hand full of ashes, sifts them through his fingers, and says, "You know Tom, I think it's fireproof now."

Even the War for Southern Independence has its moments. When asked how to spell his wife's last name, Abe Lincoln replies, "God only has one 'd' but my wife's Todd family insists on two."

We touched briefly on the medicine show, circus, and the Wild West Show. These amusements and events are a small part of our humor heritage. I know that most of our ancestors were so busy trying to eke out a living in these rocky hills that they had neither the time nor the money to travel to see these amusements. There were newspapers and word of mouth that spread stories about these spectacles.

Mark Twain

Mark Twain was America's most successful writer of colorful and humorous stories. He became internationally famous and wrote The Adventures of Huckleberry Finn which is considered the beginning of American literature. Born in Missouri he became a navigator on a steamboat that went up and down the Mississippi River. He liked the job so well that he encouraged his younger brother Henry to get a job with a steamboat line. While working on the river, Twain heard tall tales and attended many traveling minstrel shows. He loved minstrel shows.

One day a lady asked Twain if the steamboat about to carry them was going up or down. He replied: "I don't rightly know, ma'am. It's leaky and could go down, but on the other hand, as I see it, the boiler is old and rickety and it could go up."

One night Twain had a dream. He dreamed that his brother Henry was in a steamboat up river ahead of him when the thing blew up. As Henry went sailing to his death while flying over the deck where Twain was standing, to himself, Twain thought, "Hmm, maybe my idea for him to get a job on a steamboat wasn't so hot after all." A month later Henry died when a steamboat boiler exploded.

Twain loved his steamboat days on the Mississippi. The War for Southern Independence ruined the steamboat business, so he joined the Confederate Militia but left after two months. He didn't desert, he just went permanently AWOL. Wonder if he later applied for Confederate Veterans' benefits? He went to Nevada and entered the newspaper business, where on the side; he did lectures which were a forerunner of stand-up comedy.

Here are a few Mark Twain quotes:

> To succeed in life you need two things, ignorance and confidence.

> Age is an issue of mind over matter. If you don't mind, it doesn't matter.

> If you tell the truth, you don't have to remember anything.

> A man who carries a cat by the tail learns something he can learn no other way.

> Do the right thing. It will gratify some people and astonish the rest.

> In the first place, God made idiots. That was for practice. Then he made school boards.

> It's by the goodness of God that in our country we have three unspeakably precious things: freedom of speech, freedom of conscious, and the prudence to never practice either of them.

> Public servant: Person chosen by the people to distribute the graft.

> Thunder is good, thunder is impressive; but, it's lightning that does the work.

> No wonder truth is stranger than fiction. Fiction has to make sense.

Cauliflower is nothing but a cabbage with a college education.

When angry count to four, when very angry, cuss.

It's good sportsmanship to not pick up golf balls while they're still rolling. (Good advice, Mark. It could also keep you from being fitted with a circular steel golf club around your skull.)

Never let school interfere with your education.

I smoke in moderation, only one cigar at a time.
Be careful reading health books. You may die of a misprint.
Reports of my death have been greatly exaggerated.

One of the most striking differences between a cat and a lie is that a cat only has nine lives.

Honesty is the best policy when there's money in it.

Familiarity breeds contempt…and children.

It ain't what you know that gets you in trouble. It's what you know for sure that just ain't so.

Go to Heaven for the climate. Hell for the company.

Man is the only animal that blushes…or needs to.

Repartee is something we think of twenty-four hours too late.

I don't give a damn for a man that can only spell a word one way.

Clothes make the man. Naked people have little or no influence on society.

Never pick a fight with people who buy ink by the barrel.

Remember Rodney, it's easier to assassinate with ink than with lead.

Twain published U.S. Grant's memoirs, and his heirs received a quarter of a million dollars. How about that? A permanent southern AWOL publishes a winning general's memoirs and gave the heirs a fortune. You remember Grant's the one of whom General Sherman said had his back when he was crazy, and he had Grant's back when Grant was drunk.

One last word about Twain. Late in life as he was traveling the lecture circuit to pay off his debts, he began to wear white suits. I suppose you could say he was setting a precedent for Colonel Harland Sanders of Kentucky Fried Chicken fame to follow. Maybe, he was setting a precedent for Mr. Clean also.

Vaudeville began after the War for Southern Independence. There was prosperity and people had money to spend on entertainment, at least in the north. Vaudeville was a northern enterprise that used northern actors, money, and facilities because that's where the money was and that's where the culture was. If you don't believe that's where the culture was, just ask any Yankee.

I'll let the Yankees take credit for American culture. Europeans say that America is the only civilization that has risen to prominence that never produced a culture.

Tony Pastor started vaudeville in New York City. His show featured singing, dancing, trained animals, acrobats, impersonators, and comedians. It was said that any act was booked that could keep an audience's attention for three minutes.

Shortly after Pastor opened his shows in New York City, in about 1880 B.F. Keith started vaudeville in Boston. He refined the show to make it more gentile than the bawdy minstrel show. If an audience didn't like a minstrel show, they would stamp their feet, strike their canes against the floor, throw tomatoes, and even rush the stage. Keith had a representative from a local church to monitor acts and censor those in poor taste. His shows were for the entire family.

Keith was so successful that the Catholic Church even built ornate theaters for his shows. Vaudeville became the favorite crowd gathering place until the 1930's when movies became popular. At its height vaudeville employed twelve-thousand people and traveling shows ran all across the country. From vaudeville came the expression, "Will it play in Peoria?"

Moving Pictures, Radio, and Talkies

The first moving pictures were silent. Probably the biggest silent film star was Charlie Chaplin who liked to exercise complete control over his films by acting, directing, and writing the music for his films. He would take a film crew into an area; say a small area like this one, and with no script the crew would start filming. Let's say that he flung this rolling speaker's stand against the far wall and as he was turning to leave, it bounced back and knocked him down. If they couldn't improvise anything else humorous to film, they would wait until Charlie had another inspiration before returning to film some more. As you can see, this tended to be a long, tedious, and expensive process.

Another silent screen star was Buster Keaton. He supposedly got the name "Buster," when as a youngster; his parents were on the same bill touring with the great magician Harry Houdini. When the kid took a fall down a flight of stairs, Houdini, who saw the fall, is believed to have said, "That's a real buster." Buster became part of his parents act. Since he was constantly being thrown into the curtains, into the orchestra pit, or into the audience, for easing tossing and handling, they sewed a suitcase handle into his clothing. He was never injured, and he attributed it to his being limp during the fall and breaking it with a hand or a foot. He was known as the "great stone face" for his deadpan expression. His best movie was *The General*.

Another silent screen star during this era was Harold Lloyd. He was known for physical comedy and his stunt performances. He lost a thumb and an index finger on his right hand when he mistook a bomb for a prop that blew up while he was attempting to light a cigarette from the fuse. Wonder if he got the cigarette lit, and did he inhale? He wore a prosthetic glove in films thereafter.

The first motion picture with sound starred Al Jolson in The Jazz Singer. "Mammy Mammy." Jolson was supposedly the greatest entertainer who ever lived and if folks didn't believe that he was the greatest entertainer who ever lived, all they had to do was ask him. On stage he was an ocean of energy. His energy on stage made the Energizer Battery Bunny look like a sleepwalker.

He performed in the day before microphones and state of the art sound systems. At that time I think the idea was for a stage actor or actress to use their voice to strip the paint off the wall behind the audience seated in the back row of the balcony. He not only sang and danced but told jokes, also. Supposedly, while playing Broadway in New York, he would attend other shows and with a pencil and paper, he would jot down gags he liked from other comedians to use in his show. He would then have his lawyer to write the gag originator a letter to cease using the jokes because they belonged to Jolson. What's not to like about a guy like that?

Once Bing Crosby saw Jolson in Seattle, Washington, and described his performance as electric. Of course, as laid back as Bing was, I'm sure that he would have considered Jolson's breathing to be electric.

The Jazz Singer movie was loosely based on Al Jolson's life. The starring role was offered first to George Jessel who played the part on Broadway, but he turned it down because Warner Brothers owed him money from previous films. Eddie Cantor also turned down the part probably for the same reason since the movie business in those days worked on a shoestring which sometimes broke. Since Warner Brothers lacked funds for the project, Al Jolson became the star and main backer of the film. This first "talkie" became a huge box office success.

Jolson once said, "I'll tell you when I'm going to play the palace. (The palace was the Mecca for a vaudeville performer.) That's when Eddie Cantor and George Burns and Groucho Marx and Jack Benny are on the bill. I'm going to buy out the whole house and sit in the middle of the orchestra and say, 'Slaves, entertain; the king.'" As you can surmise Al was a modest man. His favorite saying was, "You ain't heard nothing yet."

From vaudeville came W.C. Fields, Mae West, Buster Keaton, the Marx Brothers, Jimmy Durante, Bill "Bojangles" Robinson, Edgar Bergen, Fanny Brice, Burns and Allen, Eddie Cantor, and others. Also, from vaudeville came a cowboy by the name of Will Rogers. He would twirl a rope while telling jokes, and he loved to say, "All I know is what I read in the papers." He was an avid proponent of air travel and wouldn't you know, he died in a plane crash in Alaska.

Here are some of Will's tidbits of wisdom:

> Be thankful we're not getting all the government we're paying for.

Communism is like prohibition, it's a good idea but it won't work.

The only time a person dislikes gossip is when its about him.

There's no trick to being a humorist. You've got the whole government working for you.

I belong to no organized political party, I'm a democrat.

Everything is changing. People are taking their comedians seriously and their politicians as a joke.

W.C. Fields was born in Philadelphia and ran away from his father at an early age. He became a juggler in vaudeville and later performed comedy in talking movies. He learned talking out of the side of his mouth from his mother. Here are a few of Fields favorite lines:

A rich man is a poor man with money.

Everything I do is either illegal, immoral, or fattening.

Marriage is better than leprosy because it's easier to get rid of.

I cook with wine, sometimes I even add it to the food.

I spent half my money on gambling, alcohol and women. The other half I wasted.

If I had my life to live over, I'd live over a liquor store.
I once spent a year in Philadelphia, I think it was on a Sunday.

Nothing like a mink coat. It will not only keep a girl warm, it'll keep her quiet.

I never hold a grudge. As soon as I get even, I forget it.

"Lady, did anybody ever tell you that you were a vision of beauty?"
"Oh my, Mr. Fields."
"They were lying."

Women are like elephants. I like to look at 'em, but I wouldn't want to own one.

I like children, fried.

A woman drove me to drink and I didn't have the decency to thank her.

Ah, the patter of little feet around the house. There's nothing like having a midget for a butler.

I don't trust doctors. The one down the street treated a man nine years for jaundice. Come to find out the patient was a Korean.

It was said of Fields that any man who hates dogs and children can't be all bad. If W.C. were alive today, I wonder if he would say, "I got a bang out of my next door neighbor, he was an Islamic Jihadist."

The biggest laugh W.C. ever got was when a tray of dishes inadvertently fell backstage during one of his performances. When the noise finally stopped with the last little tinkle what seemed like thirty minutes later, he whispered, "Mice."

Mae West was born in Brooklyn, New York, and wrote plays and performed on Broadway. She went to Hollywood to make pictures when she was in her early forties. In New York City she was once sentenced to jail for two weeks for producing and staging an obscene play entitled, Sex. She dined with the warden and his wife, and believe me, that's punishment. When asked if she believed in censorship, she replied: "I certainly do. It's made me a fortune."

In her first movie *Night after Night* with George Raft, she rewrote her scene. In that scene the hatcheck girl says, "Goodness, what a beautiful mink coat," to which Mae replies, "Goodness had nothing to do with it." Raft said she stole everything in the movie but the cameras. In 1935 and now a successful movie star, she spotted handsome Cary Grant in a waiting room and to her movie director, she says, "I'll take him, if he can talk."

In World War II air crews had life preservers affectionately called Mae West's.

Here are some West Lines:

> I like two kinds of men; domestic and imported.
> When I'm good I'm very good, but when I'm bad I'm better.
> She's the kind of girl who climbed the ladder of success…
>   wrong by wrong.

A man in the house is worth two on the curb.

It's not the men in my life that counts. It's the life in my men.

Too much of a good thing…can be wonderful.

Why don't you come up and see me sometime…when I've got nothing on but the radio.

When a girl goes wrong, men go right…after her.

I used to be Snow White but I drifted.

Give a man a free hand and he'll run it all over you.

If Mae were alive today, I wonder if she would say, "I don't mind standing in line for punch so long as nobody steals my punch line," or "I can handle a mean man if he is a man of means."

Groucho Marx and the Marx Brothers were born in New York City to Jewish immigrant parents. The Marx brothers started as a singing group and were touring the vaudeville circuit but were only an average act. While performing in Nacogdoches, Texas, a team of runaway horses drew the audience from their performance. While the auditorium was more or less empty, they began clowning around by doing a comedy routine, probably being themselves. The audience that was filing back in liked them so much that they changed their act from singing to comedy.

Here are a few of Groucho's quotes:

I wish you would keep my hands to yourself.

Women should be obscene and not heard.

Who are you going to believe, me or your lying eyes.

We took pictures of the native girls, but they weren't developed. We're going back next year.

Politics doesn't make strange bedfellows, marriage does.

Paying alimony is like feeding hay to a dead horse.

Anyone who says he can see through a woman is missing a lot.

One morning I shot an elephant in my pajamas. How he got in my pajamas I'll never know.

A man's only as old as the woman he feels.

Blood's not thicker than money.

A few years ago I made a killing on Wall Street. I shot a broker.

I don't care to belong to any club that would have me as a member.

If Groucho were still around, I would try to run this one by him. Problems are simple once you work the complications out. The Marx Brothers made a number of zany movies together. Margaret Dumont was the leading lady in their films, and she became known as the fifth Marx Brother.

Raspy voiced Jimmy Durante was a singer, pianist, and comedian who made it into radio in the 1940's. He dropped out of school in the seventh grade to become a ragtime pianist. He would break into a song and deliver a joke with orchestral punctuation after each line. His vaudeville act included him leading a white elephant across the stage. Someone would ask, "Where are you going with that elephant?" He would reply, "What elephant?"

Here are some of Durante's lines:

> Man is the only animal that can be skinned more than once.
> My wife has a slight speech impediment. Every now and then she stops to breathe.
> Politics is developing more comedians than show business ever did.
> When I was through with him he was covered in blood. My blood.

He poked humor at his nose which he called a snozola. He said phrases like, "Dat's my boy," and "I got a million of 'em." He would end his show, by saying, "Good night Mrs. Calabash, wherever you are."

George Burns and Gracie Allen were a comedy duo that toured the vaudeville circuit. George had several partners, and he said that his act wasn't funny until Gracie became his partner. He learned early that Gracie could get more laughs as a straight man than he could by delivering the punch lines. They switched roles, with George writing most of the material, and they became a sensation.

Gracie was born in San Francisco. She was born with a condition called heterochromia, or two different color eyes, one blue and one green. She told a reporter that she was born in December 1906 after the big July earthquake, but he could not find a record of her birth. When he asked her about it, she replied, "Well, it was a mighty big earthquake." In 1940 as a gag, she announced that she was running for President on the Surprise Party ticket. To her and everyone's surprise she received 42,000 votes.

Here are a few Burns and Allen lines:

> George, when I was young all the men slept in the same bed. Let's see, there was my father, my brothers, my nephew, cousin, and my uncle.
> Gracie, I'm surprised your grandfather didn't sleep with them too.
> Oh, he did but he died and they made him get up.

> Gracie, what are you doing bringing all those flowers home?
> You told me to visit your mother and take some flowers.

Gracie and George had a radio program for several years. Gracie retired and George performed solo.

Here are some of George's lines:

> Nice to be here. At my age it's nice to be anywhere.

By the time you're eighty you've learned everything. Now, if only you can remember it.

I never looked better, felt better, made love better, and I'll tell you something else. I've never lied better.

I'd announce that I was going to sing, and all the guests would make a ring around the piano. But somehow I managed to fight my way through the ring and sing anyway.

Happiness: A good cigar, a good meal, and a good woman... or a bad woman; it depends on how much happiness you can take.

You're getting old when you stoop down to tie your shoelaces and wonder what else you can do while you're down there.

I was brought up to respect my elders, so now I don't have to respect anybody.

No snowflake in an avalanche ever feels responsible.

When I was a boy the Dead Sea was only sick.

The secret of a good sermon is to have a good beginning and a good ending and have the two as close together as possible.

Sincerity...if you can fake that, you've got it made.

Happiness is having a large loving, caring, close-knit family in another city.

Making love at ninety is like trying to shoot pool with a rope.

(Hey George, ever hear of John Shell from Louisville, Kentucky. Remember, he's the one who died at one-hundred-thirty-four, had a ninety-year-old son and seven-year-old son.)

Eddie Cantor was a singer, dancer, songwriter, and comedian. He starred on a radio variety show called the Chase and Sanborn Hour in 1931 and became known as "The Captain of Comedy." He performed on radio programs until the early 1950's.

George Jessel was called the Toastmaster General of the United States. He was emcee at numerous gatherings and conventions. George once said the human brain starts working the minute you're born and never stops until you stand up to make a speech.

African-American characters Amos and Andy became a radio sensation. Freeman Gosden was born in Richmond, Virginia, and was an army radio operator in World War I. Charles Correll was from Peoria, Illinois, and the two met in Durham, N.C. These white men were in radio, first with a program called Sam and Henry, and in 1928 they changed it to Amos and Andy. Originally, they voiced all the characters on the radio program but later expanded to include other performers. In the early 1950's the television version of Amos and Andy, with an all African-American cast, had a short run but was canceled due to complaints by the NAACP. Should it have been white characters in blackface?

Years later, Freeman said the reason they chose black characters was because blackface comics could tell funnier stories than white comics. I suppose blackface added more rhythm to their humor.

Fred Allen was an American comedian who starred in radio's golden age from 1934–1949. After radio he became a hit on Tallulah Bankhead's The Big Show. He was famous for his ad libs, and his comedy was the standard that other radio comedians tried to equal. His shows included Town Hall Tonight and later the Fred Allen Show.

Here are some Fred Allen lines:

> TV is called the new medium. That's because nothing is done well.

> TV allows people who have nothing to do to watch people who can't do anything.

> I like long walks, especially when they are taken by people who annoy me.

> The first time I sang in a church choir two-hundred people changed their religion.

> Committee; A group of men who individually can do nothing but as a group decide nothing can be done.

> The first thing that strikes a visitor in Paris is a cab.

> I don't have to look up my family tree, because I know I'm the sap.
>
> •

> Popularity has the life expectancy of a small boy looking into a gas tank with a lighted match.

I play a musical instrument a little, but for my own amazement.
The last time I saw him he was walking down lover's lane holding his own hand.

A committee is a group of the unprepared, appointed by the unwilling to do the unnecessary.

Most of us spend six days a week sowing wild oats; then we go to church on Sunday and pray for crop failure.

An income tax form is like a laundry list, either way you lose your shirt.
I just returned from Boston. It's the only thing to do if you find yourself up there.

I can't understand why a person will spend a year to write a novel when he can easily buy one for a couple of bucks.

I don't want to own anything that won't fit into my coffin.
Hollywood is a place where people from Iowa mistake each other for stars.
A telescope can magnify a star a thousand times, but a good press agent can do even better.
Ed Sullivan will be around as long as someone else has talent.

Imitation is the sincerest form of TV.

My uncle is a southern planter. He's an undertaker in Alabama.

The Jack Benny Show ran from 1932–1955. Jack was a master of comedic timing and played an eternally thirty-nine-year-old skinflint. A famous gag from his show is that Jack was going home one night when a man asks for a light. The man then says: "This is a stick up. Now come on, your money or your life." Pause. "I said, your money or your life?" Pause. "Look bud, I said your money or your life?" Jack says, "I'm thinking, I'm thinking."

Lum and Abner was a radio program based on a backwoods hillbilly theme. Lum Edwards was played by Chester Lauck, and Norris Goff played Abner Peabody who ran the Jot 'Em Down Store. These two University of Arkansas graduates from the state of Arkansas started out in blackface but decided on a hillbilly theme before they landed a network radio show in 1931. They wrote the first scripts and voiced several of the characters.

Fibber McGee and Molly was a big radio show. Jim and his wife, Marian Driscoll Jordan, were from Peoria, Illinois. Jim entertained troops in France during WWI and after the war he tried vaudeville solo. Later Jim and Marian did vaudeville together for a while with limited success. When Jim was visiting his brother in Chicago, they were listening to a radio program when Jim bet his brother ten dollars that he and Marian could do better than the characters they were hearing. Jim won the bet and their show ran from 1931–1959. It featured a clustered hall closet as a running gag. The show gave us expressions like, "That ain't the way I heard it!" And "Tain't funny McGee." A Molly McGee quote: When a man brings you flowers for no reason…there's a reason.

Art Linkletter was born, Gordon Arthur Kelly. He was abandoned by his Canadian parents, raised by a preacher, and later became a U.S. citizen in 1942. He worked for the KGB, that's the call letters of a radio station in San Diego, California. He did a radio show called People Are Funny and later a show by the same name on TV. He invested and promoted the hula hoop. He was married for almost 65 years…to the same woman. Well, in Hollywood you have to qualify marriage. Here are a three of Art's lines: I'm asked by kids why I condemn marijuana when I haven't tried it. The greatest obstetricians in the world have never been pregnant. A finished product is one that has already seen its better days.

Singer Kate Smith had a radio variety show from 1937–1945. She was five feet ten inches tall, weighed two-hundred-thirty-five pounds, and never married. She popularized the song "God Bless America."

Eve Arden was born in Mill Valley, California, in 1908. At the age of sixteen she left high school to join a stock theater and later the Ziegfield Follies in 1934. She had a husky voice and played bit parts in several movies and TV shows. Eve portrayed English teacher Connie Brooks from 1948–1957 in the radio series Our Miss Brooks. She was made an honorary member of the NEA and received job offers to teach. Only in America can a high school dropout like Eve get job offers to teach. One of Eve's quotes: Treat a horse like a woman and a woman like a horse and they'll both win for you.

Edgar Bergen was born in Chicago to Swedish parents. He was an actor, comedian, and ventriloquist. On radio programs from

1937–1956, he had several dummies, two of which were Charley McCarthy and Mortimer Snerd. He was married to Frances Westerman and had a daughter, Candice, who was known as Charley McCarthy's sister. Here are three of Edgar's quotes: The only man who sticks closer to you in adversity than a friend is a creditor. When my boss asked me who is the stupid one me or him, I told him everyone knows he doesn't hire stupid people. Show me where Stalin is buried and I'll show you a communist plot.

Fanny Brice was born in New York City and sang in vaudeville. She was a comedienne that acted in the movies. She had several hit songs, one of which was "My Man." She liked to sing so well that she married her second husband, Julius W. "Nicky" Arnstein, who spent fourteen months in Sing Sing. I suppose you could say that this song bird married a jail bird. She made it big on radio by starring in Baby Snooks and Daddy from 1937–1951. When the show began she was a forty-seven-year-old who voiced a bratty nine-year-old girl. Try twenty-one minutes of sounding like a nine-year-old kid sometime. Yeah, I know, a second childhood can do wonders but not one like that. Here is a Fanny quote: Men always fall for frigid women because they put on the best show.

You may have never heard of Henry Morgan, but I do want to mention him. In 1940 Morgan had a fifteen minute radio series where he opened the program by saying, "Good evening, anybody; here's Morgan." That was in response to Kate Smith's saying; "Good evening, everybody" which he thought was condescending. His specialty was antagonizing sponsors of which an early one was Adler Shoe Stores. He made a reference to old man Adler on the air and was almost canceled, but when people went into stores and asked to see old man Adler, he backed off. Adler came out with a fall line of colors that Morgan thought was horrible and on the air, he said, "I wouldn't wear them to a dogfight, but perhaps our listeners will like them." The old man demanded an on-air apology. Morgan obliged by saying, "I would wear them to a dogfight." This apology evidently made the old man happy.

He moved to ABC and was sponsored by Oh Henry candy bars. He said, "Try one. Eat two and your teeth will fall out." He altered a Schick injector blade slogan that was, "Push-pull; click-click" to "Push-pull; nick-nick." Life Savers candy accused him of fraud. The company dropped him when he accused them of hiding the holes. "If the manufacturer would give me all those centers," he said, "I would market them as Morgan's Mint Middles." He described the mint middles as cement, asphalt, and asbestos flavored. He won a Peabody Award in 1946 while on ABC.

One movie duo was Stan Laurel and Oliver Hardy. Stan Laurel was born in Lancashire, England, and was Charlie Chaplin's understudy. He was known for his whiny face and was once asked if he had any bad habits, to which he replied, "Yes, I married them all." He wrote and edited the movies he and Oliver Hardy made and once said that if anyone cried at his funeral he would never speak to them again. In Hollywood his telephone number was listed in the telephone book. Oliver Hardy was from Harlem…Harlem, Georgia, and was the son of a Confederate Veteran. Once asked if he was happy with the arrangement of his partner making a larger salary for their movies, he replied to the effect, why shouldn't I, he's doing all the work. This is one of the few comic duo teams where one partner genuinely liked the other.

In a second wave from vaudeville came Jack Benny, Abbott and Costello, Kate Smith, Cary Grant, Bob Hope, Milton Berle, Judy Garland, Rose Marie, Sammy Davis Jr., Red Skelton, and The Three Stooges.

Movie theaters, as I recall, had a couple of animated cartoons shown prior to the feature film. Walt Disney created the first animated cartoon with a black mouse named, Mickey, and his success was followed by a number of others by different creators. These cartoons relied on physical humor with some wordplay.

In the 30's and 40's short animated cartoons were followed by fifteen to twenty minute humorous shorts. These twenty minute shorts were generally The Three Stooges, the most famous and notorious of the shorts. Moe Howard was the leader of the group and was fourth of five brothers who were born in Brooklyn, New York, to Lithuanian Jewish parents. The Brooklyn accent in their dialogue tends to make their comedy funnier. Words like "work" became woerk, and murder became moerder, etc. This comedy act was under the guidance of Ted Healy at the beginning of their career. There was always a trio in their short films, and each actor was paid six-hundred dollars per week. The actors were: Larry, Moe, and Shemp Howard, and later a younger brother, Jerome "Curly," replaced Shemp. They made one-hundred-ninety shorts and, according to critics, their "slapstick" comedy violated almost ever rule of comedy. Well, they made folks laugh.

Harry Cohn of Columbia pictures kept the group with Moe as the leader on a leash. He gave them one year contracts at a salary of seven-thousand-five-hundred dollars per film to be divided among the trio. He didn't increase their salary when they became widely popular because he constantly told Moe that demand for shorts was waning. However, theater chains were informed by Cohn that to get Stooge shorts they had to show B movies that were in little demand. That's one way to keep a good act going, keep them hungry.

Abbott and Costello made thirty-six feature length movies between 1940–1956. Bud Abbott was the straight man, getting sixty percent for performing, while Lou Costello got forty percent. Later Lou demanded fifty percent and finally sixty percent. Nothing like playing the percentages I always say. Bud Abbott's parents worked in the Barnum and Bailey Circus. While growing up Lou Costello played basketball, and later in Hollywood he became an occasional stuntman. He left Hollywood to perform comedy with Bud Abbott in burlesque, vaudeville, and minstrel shows. Thanks to their films they became the highest paid duo in the world during World War II. Both were big spenders, avid gamblers, and developed IRS problems in the 50's. They split in 1956 and Costello died in 1959. The pair never played baseball but were honored by a plaque in Cooperstown's Baseball Hall of Fame for their "Who's on First" routine. Groucho Marx called Bud Abbott the greatest straight man ever.

From 1947–1957 Universal Studios cast Marjorie Main and Percy Kilbride as a hillbilly duo, Ma and Pa Kettle. This movie duo had fifteen kids frolicking in ten feature length movies. It was Marjorie Main, who said, "A woman never forgets the man she could have married; a man, the woman he couldn't."

From 1949–1956 Dean Martin and Jerry Lewis made sixteen films. Jerry Lewis, whom the French believe to be a comic genius, grew up with a vaudeville father and a mother who played the piano. He later taught film directing classes at Southern California and two of his students were Steven Spielberg and George Lucas. Here are three of Jerry's lines: Every man's dream is to sink into a woman's arms without falling into her hands. I've had great success being a total idiot. I have some very personal feelings about politics, but I don't get into it because I do comedy already.

Dean Martin was born of Italian parents in Steubenville, Ohio. He dropped out of high school in the tenth grade because he thought he was smarter than the teachers. He bootlegged liquor, served as a speakeasy croupier, was a blackjack dealer, worked in a steel mill, and boxed as a welterweight. At fifteen he received a broken nose from boxing and because he couldn't afford tape, Martin broke the knuckles on his hands. About his boxing career he stated that he had twelve bouts and won all but eleven. He was singing in nightclubs as Dino Martini where he met Jerry Lewis who was also on the bill. Here are two of Dean's lines: You're not drunk if you're in the floor and don't need to hold on. I've got seven kids. The words I get around my house are "hello," "goodbye," and "I'm pregnant."

From 1940--1957 Bob Hope, born in London, England, and Bing Crosby, born in Tacoma, Washington, made a series of road films that some believe were supposed to be funny. Bing once said, "There's not a thing in the world I wouldn't do for Hope and there's not a thing in the world he wouldn't do for me…we spend our lives not doing a thing for each other." Bob Hope hired an army of writers to help with his lines. In fact, it was said that as a baby he wouldn't speak to his parents until writers were hired for him.

Here are some Hope lines:

> You know you're getting old when the candles cost more than the cake.
> Middle age is when your age starts to show around our middle.
> A bank will lend you money if you can prove you don't need it.
>
> I grew up with six brothers. That's how I learned to dance… waiting for the bathroom.
> She said she was approaching forty; I couldn't help wondering from which direction.
> The trees in Siberia are miles apart, that is why the dogs run so fast.
> Bigamy is the only crime where two rites make a wrong.

While these performers were entertaining us, who was entertaining them? Some of them followed the exploits of George Herman "Babe" Ruth whose towering homeruns transformed the game of baseball. A reporter once asked him why he made more money than President Hoover, to which the Babe replied, "I'm doing more than he is." Babe was the son of German immigrants and was called "Bambino" which I thought was Italian. Go figure.

To me the Babe was larger than life. I think of him as having six hands and six arms. Two hands hold a baseball bat, the next two to hold a beer in one hand and a hot dog in the other, and the third set is to hold a woman in each arm. Maybe that's why they called him Babe.

And there was Enrico Caruso the great Italian opera singer. I know our folks probably couldn't afford a ticket to see him while he was on tour and wouldn't have enjoyed his singing anyway. They had no appreciation of singers on stage who went screaming to their death. Oh, but they loved to laugh while aping and opera singer. Caruso was in the 1906 San Francisco earthquake.

My candidate for the person entertaining the entertainers is Tallulah Bankhead. This husky voiced actress was born in Huntsville, Alabama, into the powerful Bankhead and Brockman family. Her grandfather was U.S. Senator John H. Bankhead, she was the niece of U.S. Senator John H. Bankhead II, and was the daughter of U.S. Representative William Brockman Bankhead. Her mother died of blood poisoning when she was a month old, and she was reared mostly by her grandmother, Tallulah James Brockman Bankhead, in Jasper, Alabama. She was sent to various schools in a vain attempt to keep her out of trouble.

In the south there was a common joke. Mothers would lock-up their daughters to keep them away from bad boys when they came around. Well, when Tallulah came home from boarding school to her grandmother's house in Jasper, Alabama, mothers would hide their sons from Tallulah. I'd say that's equality in the hiding of the sexes.

She won a beauty contest at an early age and went to New York City. Unable to get a start in New York theaters, she went to England and became a hit on the London stage. In a London play a monkey in her arms grabbed a wig off her head, went down into the footlights, and waved it in front of the audience. The audience howled with laughter, but not to be out done, Tallulah did cartwheels across the stage. The audience loved it.

She called everyone "dahling." She pronounced darling, dahling because she couldn't remember names. Wish it could work for me but calling everybody dahling doesn't quite have the right ring for my intentions. I'm afraid to try it. She smoked seven packs of cigarettes a day and said that cocaine wasn't habit-forming. She said she knew it wasn't habit-forming because she had used it for years. She once saw an old boyfriend that she hadn't seen in several years. To him, she said, "Dahling, I thought I told you to wait in the car." She also said: "If I had my life to do over I'd make the same mistakes, only sooner. Nobody can be me. Even I have trouble doing it."

Gossip columnist Earl Wilson once asked her, "Have you ever been mistaken for a man on the phone?" "No," she replied, "have you?" Twenty-seven-year-old Helen Hayes was about to get married and asked Tallulah how to keep from getting in the family way. "Dahling," Tallulah replied, "do what you've always been doing." She was notorious for wearing no panties and doing cartwheels at parties.

Oh! That's a tumbleweed. For a minute I thought it was Tallulah Bankhead turning cartwheels.

Here are some Tullulah lines:

"What! No toilet paper," she once said to a barkeeper. "Got two fives for a ten?"

They filmed, Shirley Temple, through gauze. They should have filmed me through linoleum.

I'm as pure as the driven slush.

Only good girls keep diaries. Bad girls don't have time.

I'll come and make love to you at five o'clock. If I'm late, start without me.

While filming *Lifeboat* she climbed a ladder and flashed the cast and film crew. They complained to director Alfred Hitchcock who replied, "I don't know if it is a problem with wardrobe or hair dressing." For Bette Davis, Tallulah had no love, and she said: "That hag's been spreading gossip about me. When I get hold of her I'll tear out every hair of her mustache." She was married once and had four abortions.

In 1936 her father became speaker of the U.S. House of Representatives. She, at the height of her fame, or notoriety, called him up, and said: "Oh papa, dahling, it's wonderful. I'm so happy for you. Now, don't you do anything to embarrass me." Somebody once described Tallulah as and orgy on two legs. Well, today, do you know any girls named Tallulah? In my opinion, if anyone does name a child Tallulah, Disney women Lindsay Lohan and Miley Cyrus could be two likely candidates. So, my choice for the entertainer entertaining the entertainers is Tallulah Bankhead.

Television came along in the 1950's. Milton Berle, the first big TV star, became known as "Mr. Television" and signed a lifetime contract with NBC that lasted for several years. Milton refused to die except while performing, so they reduced his air time. He was born Mendel Berlinger in Harlem to Jewish parents, Moses and Sarah Berlinger. He became a stand-up comic who patterned his act after Ted Healy and starred on the Milton Berle radio show from 1947–1948. In 1948 he went to television on Tuesday evenings with the Texaco Star Theater where he revived most of his old vaudeville routines. He made TV popular.

Berle, we're considering canceling your lifetime contract. We have grounds because on set you've already died five times.

Leading the laughter and cheering for Milton was his mother. She was a plant in the studio audience, and one night she raised the roof with laughter when he appeared in a silly costume, which prompted Milton to say: "Lady, you've got all night to make a fool of yourself. I only have one hour." He was accused of stealing jokes from other comedians which he embraced. Walter Winchell called Berle "The thief of bad gags."

Cheer up, darling! Milton Berle says the flood will give the town a million dollars worth of improvements. (1940 flood)

Here are some Milton Berle quotes, maybe:

A committee is a group that keeps minutes and loses hours.

We owe a lot to Edison…if it wasn't for him we'd be watching television by candlelight.

If evolution works how come mothers only have two hands?

Experience is what you have after you've forgotten her name.

A good wife always forgives her husband when she's wrong.

Jews don't drink much because it interferes with their suffering.

Berle did more charity shows than Bob Hope. They weren't as high profile.

I love Lucy began to air on CBS in 1951. The idea was formed by a 1948 radio program in which Lucille Ball played a wacky wife. She insisted on her band-leader husband, Dezi Arnaz, playing in the TV show also, but the network balked against a Cuban actor appearing on American TV, so the pair toured the country in vaudeville venues. The show became so successful that in 1953 twenty-nine million saw Ike sworn in as President, and forty-four million saw Lucy Ricardo welcome her new baby. It was one of the most successful situation comedies ever which is pretty good for a girl kicked out of acting class due to stage fright. Earlier, in 1942 brown haired Lucille ball became a redhead at MGM's insistence.

Here are some Lucille lines:

The secret of staying young is to live honestly, eat slowly, and lie about your age.

> You see much more of your children once they leave home.

> I'm not funny, I'm just brave.

> How was I Love Lucy born? We decided that instead of divorce lawyers profiting from our mistakes, we'd profit from them.

A Dezi Arnaz quote: My problem with comedy is that I don't understand the jokes.

The Red Skelton Show ran from 1951–1970. It featured Red playing various comic characters, and he always wanted to be thought of as a clown. He wrote music, penned short stories, painted, and his art agent said that he made more money from his prints and paintings than he did as a comedian. Oh well, so much for show business.

Here are some Red lines:

> My wife runs after the garbage truck yelling, "Am I too late for the garbage?" The driver says, "No, jump in."

> I haven't spoken to my wife in eighteen months. I didn't want to interrupt her.

> I married Miss Right only to find out later that her first name was Always.

> My wife and I sleep in separate beds. Hers is in California and mine is in New Mexico.

> Our last fight was my fault. She asked, "What's on TV?" I replied, "A blanket of dust."

> She has an electric blender, electric toaster, and electric bread maker. She said, "There's so many electric gadgets there's no place to sit down." So I bought her an electric chair.

From Red's jokes one can see why he suffered financially as a comedian. Those jokes about women will get you killed on stage, screen, radio and TV. They'll get you killed anywhere, Red. Take it from me, I've had experience, I know.

Ozzie and Harriet ran from 1952–1966. It was the longest running live action sit-com in U.S. TV history. Harriet McNutt was a promising young movie actress when she met Ozzie Nelson while performing in vaudeville. Ozzie played football, attended Rutgers Law School, and coached for a while after college. He started a band and his big break came in 1930 when the New York Daily Mirror sponsored a contest to name the favorite area band. Since unsold newspapers were discarded and only the front pages were returned to the newspaper, Ozzie and his band members gathered hundreds of newspaper ballots, filed them out, and returned them to the newspaper. His band eked out Paul Whiteman's band by a few votes. You've got to love that wizard Ozzie.

Steve Allen began The Tonight Show in 1954 and hosted it until 1957. Of himself he said, "The hair is real...it's the head that's fake." Here are some more of Steve's lines: Ours is a government of checks and balances. Lobbyists write the checks and politicians improve their bank balances. My asthma seems to be in remission unless I am around cigars and dogs. I'd hate so see a dog smoking a cigar. I used to be a heavy gambler. Then I started making mental bets. That's how I lost my mind.

From 1957–1962 Jack Paar hosted The Tonight Show. Here are two of Jack's lines: Poor people have more fun than rich people, they say; and, I notice it's the rich people who keep saying it. Immigration is the sincerest form of flattery.

The situation comedy The Real McCoys ran on ABC from 1957–1962. Walter Brennan starred as Grandpa McCoy who was the head of a West Virginia family that settled in the San Fernando Valley of California. The family had two brothers named Luke, about which the older Luke said, "They were so excited, they forgot all about me."

The Andy Griffith Show ran from 1960–1968. It was set in Mayberry, a fictional town in North Carolina, and starred Andy Griffith as Sheriff Andy Taylor, and Don Knotts as his inept deputy Barney Fife. Very few law enforcement officers have escaped being compared to bungling Barney Fife. But the comparison is all in good fun, probably.

One of the highest rated TV programs of all time was The Beverly Hillbillies that ran from 1962–1971. It starred Buddy Ebsen as Jed Clampett, Irene Ryan as Granny, Donna Douglas as Jed's daughter Elly May, and Max Baer Jr. as Jed's half witted nephew Jethro Bodine. The show was created by Paul Henning. It was the first in a genre of "fish out of water" TV shows and is about a rural family who strike oil and move to Beverly Hills, California. Paul Henning wrote for Fiber McGee and Molly, Burns and Allen, The Real McCoys, and The Andy Griffith Show. Here is an Irene Ryan quote: How do you like your possum…falling off the bones tender or with a little fight left in it?

As you can see we had a rich heritage of humor ushered in by the minstrel show, vaudeville, movies, radio, and TV. In our humor heritage there are some quotes by movie stars that brought a smile to our ancestors' faces.

For instance, Errol Flynn is an Australian actor who became a U.S. citizen in 1942. This swashbuckling star of Robin Hood and other fast paced motion pictures portrayed a man of action on the screen that could swish a sword easier than Bette Davis could swing a cigarette. In 1942 as a new U.S. citizen, he volunteered to join the army to serve in World War II. You know, except for a bad back, TB, several venereal and heart diseases, I think that he would have been inducted.

There's a given in Hollywood. Studios will never publicize the true facts about their screen stars. Take Rock Hudson; I never thought a thing about him holding his leading lady and romantic interest to one side and talking her to death, not until years later. For him to make passionate love to an actress on the silver screen would have been an Oscar worthy performance. Studios kept us in the dark.

Anyway, Errol Flynn said, "It isn't what people say about you, it's what they whisper." Errol, I believe that in your case there was plenty to whisper about.

Bette Davis, who survived in Hollywood long enough to become a star, said: "I was brought up to respect the conventions; love had to end in marriage. I'm afraid mine did." She also said, "Old age is no place for sissies." Bette proved that on the silver screen, raging 'bitchy' has more box-office appeal than raving beauty.

Cary Grant once said everybody wants to be Cary Grant; even I want to be Cary Grant. He married five times, and in 1942 he married the world's richest woman, Betty Hutton of the E.F. Hutton and Woolworth fortune. He resented the couple being called Cash and Cary. He said that divorce is a game played by lawyers.

Joan Crawford, who hit the spot by marrying, among others, the head of Pepsi-Cola said: "Love is a fire. But you don't know if it is going to warm your hearth or burn your house down." I think the way Joan raised her kids was the inspiration for Dr. Benjamin Spock to write the book *Child and Baby Care*.

Katharine Hepburn said, "If you want to sacrifice the admiration of many men for the criticism of one, go ahead, get married."

Elizabeth Taylor; it wasn't a magazine until her picture was on the cover. She collected eight husbands and one-hundred-fifty million dollars worth of jewelry; in fact, she had more ice than an Alaskan glacier. She was born with a genetic mutation called distichiasis, which translated means she had two sets of eyelashes. She was hospitalized seventy times, had twenty major operations, and her best performances were acting as though nothing was the matter with her. She said some of her best leading men were dogs and horses.

Mickey Rooney was five feet two inches tall and was married eight times. He could sing, dance, clown, and play musical instruments. He could do about anything but keep a wife. He would have made a great stand-up comic had the audience been able to see him.

Here are some of Mickey's quotes:

> Always get married in the morning. That way if it doesn't work out, you haven't wasted the whole day.
> I'm five foot two inches tall, but I was seven foot tall when I married Ava Gardner.

> People ask me how short I am. Since my last divorce, I'm a quarter million short.
> Alimony is like pumping gas into another man's car.

> I lost two dollars at the Santa Anita race track and I've spent three million trying to get it back.

Marilyn Monroe said that Hollywood is a place where they'll pay you a quarter of a million dollars for a kiss and fifty cents for your soul. This natural brunette was no ordinary dumb blonde.

Ava Gardner was discovered while she was visiting a sister in New York City. Louis B. Mayer saw an audition reel of her and to his New York agent, he said, "Al, she can't sing, she can't act, she can't talk, she's terrific." Ava said, "Deep down I'm pretty superficial." Helen of Troy's was a face that launched a thousand ships while Ava's was a face that Frank Sinatra chased all over the world.

Publisher and humorist Bennett Cerf said, "Middle age is when your classmates are so gray and wrinkled and bald they don't recognize you."

Lana Turner, who had one child and seven husbands, said: "A successful man is one who makes more money than his wife can spend. A successful woman is one who can find such a man." Also, she said, "A gentleman is a patient wolf."

Sports figures made some timely comments:

> Dizzy Dean: "They X rayed my head and found nothing."

Ted Williams divided time between playing baseball and fighting in two wars. He said, "By the time you know what to do, you're too old to do it."

Braves pitcher Johnny Sain said, "The world doesn't want to hear about labor pains, it only wants to see the baby." I'd love to have seen him running that by his wife in the maternity ward. She probably would have clubbed him with a baseball bat, but he can be forgiven. He was born in Havana. Well, he was…Havana, Arkansas.

Casey Stengel was a great Yankee manager. He said, "The secret of managing a baseball team is to keep the four guys who hate your guts away from the five guys who haven't made up their mind." And, "Without losers, where would winners be?"

At seventy-one and after being fired for blowing a World Series, Casey said, "I'll never make the mistake of being seventy again." Casey retired from baseball after he fell off a bar stool.

Mickey Mantle replaced Joe DiMaggio in center field for the Yankees. He's probably the greatest 4-F ball player to play the game of baseball. He said, "You don't realize how easy baseball is until you get up in the broadcasting booth."

Yogi Berra was a great Yankee baseball catcher. He was always good for a quote, and they're called Yogisms. Here are a few of Yogi's famous quotes:

> You can observe a lot by just watching.
> It's like deja-vu all over again.
>
> Little league baseball is a very good thing because it gets kids out of the house and parents off the streets.
>
> It was impossible to get a conversation going, everybody was talking so much.
>
> Nobody goes there anymore. It's too crowded.
>
> Baseball is ninety percent mental and the other half physical.
>
> Always go to other people's funerals, otherwise they won't come to yours.
>
> If people don't want to come to the ballpark, how are you going to stop them.
>
> Pair up in threes.
>
> I'd give my right arm to be ambidextrous.

Phil Rizzuto, Yankee shortstop and a passenger in Yogi's car, says, "Yogi, I think we're lost." "Yeah, I know," replies Yogi, "but we're making good time."

The great heavyweight champion boxer Joe Lewis was once asked who hit him the hardest. "Uncle Sam," Lewis replied.

Elvis Presley was a skinny kid from Mississippi. In 1954 he recorded a song for Sun Records in Memphis that changed the cultural landscape of this country forever. That song swept away the staid Eisenhower years of Lawrence Welk and easy listening to allow Rock and Roll to do what the "Jim Crow" song did to American culture one-hundred-nineteen years before. Elvis Presley changed the world, in my opinion, with one song.

My English teacher called it "jungle" music. Elvis had a teacher who told him he couldn't sing as did professional singer Eddie Bond, who said, "Elvis forget singing and stick to truck driving." When I first heard about Elvis driving a truck, I immediately thought of a big semi tractor and trailer rig zooming down a four lane highway. Elvis driving a little pickup was the last thing on my mind but that is what he drove. Elvis was a man dead set against illegal drugs; and yet, he thought anything a doctor prescribed was perfectly safe.

Young man I believe you'll do for country music what Bambi did for deer hunting.

This first song recorded by Elvis that changed the world was written by Arthur "Big Boy" Cradup. It was titled "That's all Right Mama." Notice the words "that's all right mama." It's giving the woman he's crazy about a license to do anything she pleases. If you've ever seen women screaming at an Elvis performance, you can believe they took those words to heart. I saw him on The Ed Sullivan Show, and I hadn't heard that much screaming and squealing since 1947 when we had a community hog killing. Why, in no time, women were burning their bras and I don't know what all.

It seems that teenagers everywhere were dancing to this new music. Some adults, though frowning outwardly, were smiling and patting their feet to this new music that Elvis performed. You should have seen some of those old fogie men folk trying to imitate the fancy footwork and those frenzied Elvis gyrations. I remember my fifty-five-year-old Uncle Max threw out his back in three places while singing the first verse of "All Shook Up." It seems that everyone was singing, smiling, and amused by the new phenomenon called Rock and Roll. Rock and Roll was the white version of Rhythm and Blues.

Our neighbor big Jake Brackens could really imitate Elvis. He was six feet four inches tall, weighted two-hundred-sixty-five pounds and was so good that Reverend McKinney was all set to have him thrown out of our Missionary Baptist Church, because, to the Reverend, it was the "Devil's" music as he called it. I remember old Jake imitating Elvis from the back of his two ton cattle truck at the Asheville Livestock Market one Thursday afternoon in July 1956. I mean, old Jake was in a big way with the gyrations, singing, scowling, sweating, and had everything going but a guitar when he pitched off the back of that parked cattle truck. He finally had to go to the French Broad River to clean the fresh cow manure from his brogans, face, and Georgia tuxedo. After that mighty fall the Reverend dropped Jake's "churching" because he never sang the Devil's music again.

Before Elvis in the 1950's, college enrollment was sixty percent men and forty percent women. Today, the numbers are reversed. There were no women U.S. Supreme Court justices and very few women legislators. Before Elvis, men opened doors for women and they still do…at their own risk.

Yes, that one song changed the world and the others by Elvis that followed reinforced it. I dare say that neither Elvis nor anyone else for that matter realized what a chain reaction this ethnic influence would have on our culture. As one musician said, "It was like opening the cell to a prison."

You can see what an explosion all the modern inventions had on our humor heritage. Within the one-hundred-seventy-five years before 1965, we came from the telegraph message that Dolly Madison sent and her being in the first official White House photograph to a cornucopia of inventions and gadgets that communicate humor and other forms of entertainment. It is astounding how we've become wired.

Just look at the inventions. Marconi invented the radio, Bell the telephone, Edison the phonograph record, Lee de Forest the tube that made TV possible, and there were other inventions and improvements on existing inventions. After the minstrel show and vaudeville, there came silent movies and then talkies, and along the way microphones were invented that amplified the sound for concert audiences that no longer required an Al Jolson type voice. For the communication of entertainment these inventions were like a cloudburst.

Recording improved. From Edison's invention came improvements like forty-five and seventy-eight rpm records, Hi-Fi, stereo, tapes, and CD players. It was an explosion that no one could have foreseen only two-hundred years ago. All of these electronic innovations have made it difficult not to communicate humor.

Newspapers made innovations like comic strips and advice columns that increased circulation. As a youngster there were a dozen or more comic strips that I enjoyed reading. I looked forward to the morning paper.

Scoop, think we'll be late with this week's paper? (1916 flood)

I'm glad that when I was growing up over fifty years ago that there were fewer restraints on what we thought was funny. We had radio, TV, movies, newspapers, and magazines that we heard, saw, or read that we passed on by word of mouth the jokes and amusing stories that enriched our humor heritage. It was a far cry from colonial days when there was almost no media communication.

In the next presentation I want to return to those good old days of yesteryear and shift our focus to our local humor. We will continue with our humor heritage right here in Madison County.

Humor Heritage Local

This is the part that most of you, I'm sure, have been anticipating. It is our local humor in Madison County that most of you have, for days, camped outside the library eagerly waiting to get inside so that you won't be turned away. By the way, for those of you who came in late, there are several empty chairs in the back row. In fact, there are vacant chairs all over the place. So let's get started.

In the first part we looked at the News-Record Digital and found humor similar to the local humor I heard growing up. Many of the jokes my father told were eerily similar to the ones in those old News-Records. My qualifications for doing humor heritage are that my mother was quick with a quip and my father could tell a tall tale.

Let me continue; I may even throw you a curve. Here are some more facts, fiction, and fantasy. Let me now shift to the humor of my youth. Every morning we received the daily paper in our mailbox, and the first thing I would read when I could snatch it away from my older brother and sisters was the comics. I suppose that Blondie was everybody's favorite and other strips included: L'il Abner, Little Orphan Annie, Archie, Mutt and Jeff, Maggie and Jiggs, Hazel, Henry, Dick Tracy, and a few more.

One of my favorite bits was a little box on the front page of the Asheville Citizen. It was called Today's Chuckle by Earl Wilson.

Here are some of Earl's pearls:

> Success is a matter of luck. Ask any failure.
> The world would be a much better place if more married couples were as deeply in love as they were in debt.
>
> Ben Franklin discovered electricity but it was the man who invented the meter who made the money.
>
> You've got to hand it to the IRS. If you don't they'll come and take it.
>
> Courage is the art of being the only one who knows you're scared to death.
>
> One way to get high blood pressure is to go mountain climbing over molehills.
> If you think nobody cares if you're alive try missing a couple of car payments.
>
> An exhaustive study of police records shows that no woman has ever shot her husband while he was doing the dishes.
>
> Gossip is when you hear something you like about someone you don't.
> Poise: The ability to be ill at ease inconspicuously.

Another feature in the newspaper was an advice column Dear Abby. I never understood what the excitement was about with her column, but the adults loved it. After researching recently

I discovered what I believe to be some of the reasons why her and other advice columns were so popular. Let me share with you a few of the letters written to advice columns.

> Dear Gertie: My husband has always boasted about being open minded, tolerant, and understanding. What makes him so abusive to me when I go out with other men?
> Dear Gertie: My boyfriend said he would die for me. But when my husband came home early from work, he ran away. Do you think my boyfriend was lying to me?
> Dear Gertie: Our unemployed son, who lives with us, moved in his girlfriend. My husband constantly drools over her and follows her like a puppy dog around the house. He can't take his eyes off her. Should I tell our son?
> Dear Gertie: My husband is a skirt chaser and cheats on me all the time. How can I be sure that the baby I'm carrying is his?
> Dear Gertie: While I work I have a new stay at home second husband. Lately he is very irritable, quarrelsome, withdrawn, disagreeable, and restless. Do you think the change could be caused by his caring for his seven adorable, young stepchildren?
> And lastly: My first husband left me twelve years ago, and he wants me to take him back. I have agreed to take him back provided it is all right with my new husband. Do you think the three of us could make it work?

One last celebrity I want to mention is Minnie Pearl. I grew up listening to the Grand Ole Opry on Saturday night, and she was one of the regulars. She would come on stage wearing a hat with a price tag marked $1.98, give a big yell, "Howdy," and the audience would cheer and applaud. She would relate some tales from the fictional town of Grinder's Switch where she claimed to be a resident. Man crazy was her persona.

Howdy! I'm so proud to be here. I'm Minnie Pearl and I want to tell you right now, I'm not boy crazy; I'm M-a-a-n crazy.

One gag she used was that her boyfriend told her that she was like a breath of spring. That's because she looked like the end of a long hard winter.

She related that a robber wanted her money and frisked her up and down. She said, "I don't have any money, but if you'll do that again I'll write you a check."

A lady spinster in Grinder's Switch died and refused to have male pallbearers. She wanted all women pallbearers. She said if the men wouldn't take her out while she was living, she wouldn't let them take her out when she was dead.

When she first started performing nobody came in the afternoon. Then at night business fell off.

A picnic is like a man's beard. You don't mind going through a little brush to get there.

Here are some expressions I would like to share with you. The first ones are from local author Sheila Adams, and they're from her book *Come Go Home With Me*. Just repeating these expressions tended to make the listener smile.

Cut the air with a dull knife.

Hot as a ginger mill.
Wore secrets like loose clothes.
Whiskey container: Thunderstorm in a bottle.

Like having the moon on your porch.
Cold as a witch's ninny pies. (At least this one is nicer than a similar one about witches and cold I heard growing up.)
Straightened her back at me.
Like fat back on a hot skillet.

Hotter than the hinges of hell.
Wore slap out.

All overs. A bad case of the all overs.

Finer than frog hair.
Smelled like yesterday's minnows.
Sullied up like a bunch of possums.
Fine as snuff and twice as dusty.

Cut didos.

Hind end of an apple cart.
Bawling like two calves in a hail storm.
Walk a rotten foot log over hell.

Nervous as a sore tailed cat in a room full of rocking chairs.

Here are some of the expressions I remember when I was growing up:

There may be snow on the roof but there's still fire in the basement.

You ain't just whistling, "Dixie."

If mama ain't happy, ain't nobody happy.

She's pretty. Pretty ugly and pretty apt to stay that way.

You might get your specs broke.

CHOMPING AT THE BIT. That has to be local or else it came from the British Isles, because I can not find chomping in the dictionary. I can find champing which means the same thing.

THUNDER STRUCK. I used that term in a theme once, and the teacher wanted to know how you could be struck by thunder. I had to agree with her. What is that Mark Twain says, thunder is impressive but it's lightning that does the work.

> Here lies the truth for it never came out.
> He's so bowlegged he couldn't hem a hog.
> You couldn't law a man off on me.

MOSSED OVER. The house is so filthy that it appears to be mossed over.

DAGMARS. Two large round front ornaments on a 1957 Chevrolet.

I'M A MONKEY'S UNCLE. That was one of my mother's favorite expressions to show mock astonishment. Like, Deacon Conrad got drunk and fell off his horse. Well, I'm a monkey's uncle. Or, rich widow Maxine Ray was taken for every cent she had by a city slicker who absconded after marrying her. Well, I'm a monkey's uncle.

HER BUG'S A WHIZZING. That was a favorite of the women folk. This expression meant that a young woman wanted to start dating and have boyfriends. I know, it sounds worse than it is.

LICK YOUR CALF OVER. That expression was used to point out to someone that they didn't do a job right the first time. They would need to do it again.

HELL AND HALF OF GEORGIA. As in, I've hunted for you all over hell and half of Georgia.

> Come hell or high water.
> Hell freezes over.

HARELIPS HELL. I'll do it if it harelips hell.

> I'd as soon be in the middle of hell with a broke back.

While we're on hell: **HELL-BENT.** That's two shades stronger than bound and determined.

Evacuate Imps! Madison County expressions
about this place is causing all
Hell to break loose.

Raise hell. That expression was used to describe someone carping because they were upset.

Ready for Morganton. Our state mental institution was located in Morganton, N.C., and this expression grew out of that. A mother would say: "You kids have driven me crazy. I'm about ready for Morganton."

Go-getter: That's a man who drives to a local radio manufacturing plant, Hammarlund, to pick up his wife after she gets off work.

See a man about a dog. I had personal experience with this one. In rural Indiana near Bedford one summer I had a flat tire and no spare. Two older country boys stopped and drove me to a service station to get the flat patched. They dropped me off, and one says: "We're going to see a man about a dog. Get your flat fixed and we'll pick you up in a few minutes." They returned four hours later, and they were reeling, pickled, and reeking. At least they remembered to come back.

The world is going to the dogs. I thought the old people who said that were nuts. I now agree with them, but how did they know? They didn't have leaders like Nancy Pelosi, Al Sharpton, Lindsey Graham, and Mitch McConnell.

At this juncture let me add something about going to the dogs. Our younger generation is trying as best they can to do the right thing and to make something of themselves. They are honest, respectful, hardworking, and try to keep the Ten Commandments. However, I'm afraid they're falling woefully short on one of the ten "Honor thy father and thy mother." They're keeping half of it and failing on the other half which I don't believe is their fault. It would help if they knew who their father was.

HAUL OFF. A song using this expression was written and performed by Wayne Raney. It was titled "Why Don't You Haul Off and Love Me." Imagine for a moment a thirty-two piece orchestra consisting of one bass fiddle and thirty-one harmonicas performing this song. Please allow me to sing the chorus.

I know that Wayne sings it better than I do, but that was the number one Hillbilly song for the year of 1947.

Another expression that made it into a song was **TOO OLD TO CUT THE MUSTARD**. I won't waste my musical talent on this ditty. I don't believe I can handle another standing ovation and demands for an encore.

As you can see, these expressions tended to put a smile on both the user and the listener's face.

A favorite past time of the men was teasing the women folk about doing a man's work. Things like instead of using a team of horses, they would suggest hitching the wife to a heavy turning plow and using her to plow a forty acre field. Another was having the lady of the house stack a truckload of hundred pound sacks of fertilizer in a barn loft. In Carter County, Tennessee, men folk defined housework as anything less than fifteen acres.

Then there were nicknames that gave fellows an extra handle. I was in a college chemistry class, and a co-ed from Baird Cove in Buncombe County called M.T. Miller, that's Joe Miller's brother, empty. There are nicknames like Shorty, Beanie, Speedy, Lightning, Foxy, etc., and if you weren't named just right, a name like Samuel Albert Parker could become SAP with the initials. And Vernon Dexter Porter became V.D. Porter. You get the idea.

Oh, another nickname is taken from News-Record Digital dated October 19, 1923. The article reads: "'Wild Bill' Anderson acquired his name by reason of his rather blustery way of talking and acting, but with it all he was usually considered rather a harmless man and was kindhearted.

"Anderson and Cy Parker argued over beans. As Parker was leaving on a mule from the Anderson property he shot Wild Bill. He died a few minutes later."

Another nickname grew out of a notorious county primary election we held in 1964. As you may recall there were some highly questionable results in a primary that included more votes cast than registered voters or county residents for that matter. A prominent local attorney was quoted in an area newspaper as saying that the election stunk so bad that a buzzard couldn't flyover the county without holding its nose. Forever after attorney James Kurtz was known by political opponents as Buzzard Kurtz.

Not long after attorney Kurtz made his observation, gag writers came out with this one: Washington is so corrupt that a buzzard flying over it spreads one wing to shield its eyes. Somehow, I have the sneaking suspicion that the Kurtz observation was picked up by professional gag writers.

So, I grew up with these colorful expressions and names. Occupants of the White House had colorful nicknames that I'm sure put smiles on our forefathers' faces.

There were names like "Long Tom" for Thomas Jefferson. It could have been "T.J. Kaleidoscope" due to the difficulty we have in pinning down his position on issues.

John Adams could have been called "Johnny One Term."

James Madison was called "Little Jimmy." His federalist enemies could have just as easily called him "Dolly's Folly."

John Quincy Adams was "The Madman of Massachusetts."

Andrew Jackson was known as "Old Hickory" but could just as easily been called "Dueling Andrew."

Martin Van Buren due to the hard times during his presidency was known as Martin Van Ruin.

William Henry Harrison was called "Old Granny."

Mr. Lincoln, how does it feel to be the only President in United States history to be called honest.

Vice President John Tyler was called "His Ascendancy" by assuming the presidency upon President William Henry Harrison's death.

James Buchanan was known as "Old Buck" and "Ten Cent Jimmy."

Abe Lincoln was called "The Rail Splitter" and "Honest Abe" among the nicer names fit to print.

Ulysses S. Grant was called "Useless."

Andrew Johnson was probably called "Impeachment the First."
Rutherford Hayes, due to how he became President, was called "His Fraudulency" and "Rutherfraud."

Grover Cleveland who weighed two-hundred-fifty pounds was known as "The Beast of Buffalo" and perhaps "Skip a term Grover."

Fancy dressing **Chester Arthur** was known as "Elegant Arthur," or "Dude"

William McKinley was known as "Wobbly Willie."

Teddy Roosevelt was known as "Old Four Eyes." Due to his dynamic energy, I probably would have called him "Animated Teddy."

William Taft was known as "Big Lub." He weighed close to three-hundred-fifty pounds, and according to urban legend he got stuck in the White House bathtub. It was said that his bathtub had stretch marks.

Woodrow Wilson was known as "The Coiner of Weasel Words," and his new wife, Edith Bolling Galt Wilson, was known after Wilson's stroke as running a "Petticoat Government." Due to his faint love for African-Americans, he could have been called "President Prejudice" or "Jim Crow Woodrow."

Warren Harding was known as "President Hardly."

It was said that **Calvin Coolidge**, "Silent Cal," was weaned on a pickle. Due to his strict eight-hour workday schedule, he could have been called "Time Clock Cal."
Franklin Roosevelt was "Houdini in the White House" and could just as easily been called "Welfare Check Franklin."

Harry Truman was known as "Give 'em hell Harry." Revisionists may want to call him "Hiroshima Harry."

John Kennedy was "Little Blue Boy."

Lyndon Johnson was "Landslide Lyndon." Johnson earned the moniker due to his winning a U.S. Senate seat by a few highly questionable votes. I wonder if Lyndon had roots in our county.

We previously mentioned Mark Twain and several media entertainers. I would like to add some more folks that our ancestors may or may not have held in high esteem.

Amelia Earhart would have been a candidate for admiration. Here was America's adored favorite early aviatrix who married at the age of thirty-four and kept her maiden name. On her wedding day she hand delivered a prenuptial note to her groom which stated that theirs was to be an open marriage. That could be why her husband became known as Mr. Earhart. Here was a woman that was flying all over the place in broad daylight and in the company of any number of male pilots and mechanics. Thanks to a favorable press there wasn't even an eyebrow raised about this behavior. What a charmed life!

Now, take our Southern Appalachian women. At this time in our history and to protect her reputation, a respectable Appalachian woman wouldn't have been seen in the company of another man except late at night on a lonely back road. Our men folk hunted deer, squirrel, and rabbit during the day; but, what separated the men from the boys in those days were those who hunted at night. These rugged mountain men stayed up all night in all kinds of weather to hunt possum, coon, and fox. These night hunters were serious because they hunted on far steep mountains, sloping hills, and grassy valleys, not so much to find possum, coon, and fox, but to find parked on lonely back roads those souls who were poaching beaver. Finding and reporting the right beaver baggers could fuel a local gossip mill for a full decade.

Amelia basked in fame while flying as free as a falcon all over the place. She got so good and confident about her flying that she sawed off her plane's ugly, unwieldy radio antenna with a dull hacksaw blade.

> In 1937 after flying almost around the world, her male co-pilot looked over the vast blue sea and sky expanse of the South Pacific, and said, "Amelia, there's no more radio contact. I think we're lost."
> Amelia replies, "We may be lost but flying beats the devil out of housework."

That Amelia Earhart; she flew for six years after her marriage, and they spent the next sixty years looking for her. Had that been a Southern Appalachian woman, we would have labeled her "that kind of woman" and forgotten about her. But, as we were fond of saying back then, "That's life."

Another pilot who made a name for himself was Charles Lindbergh. In 1927 Charles Lindbergh, a.k.a. Carieu Kent, was the first man to fly solo across the Atlantic to win the $25,000

Orteig Prize. He became an instant celebrity, and New York City honored him with a ticker tape parade. Lindbergh flew around the country where he was seen by one quarter of the American population. He was more famous than the astronauts who later rocketed to and walked on the moon. He said he didn't want to be like those other fly-boys barnstorming across the country and womanizing a long the way. Lindbergh said there would be no "facile" relationships for him. I assume by facile he meant one-night stands. In 1929 he met and married our Mexican ambassador's daughter Anne Morrow and together they had five children. He was a hero for a whole generation. He passed away in 1974.

What about the alias Carieu Kent? Between 2003–2005 it was revealed by German newspapers and a biographer that Charles Lindbergh, using the alias Carieu Kent, had fathered seven children by three different mistresses who never married. These trysts with younger single women began when he was in his early fifties. So, in the early 2000's our fly-boy became a hero all over again to a whole new generation. With these new revelations I think we ought to have, in his honor, another ticker tape parade. Like he said, he didn't believe in facile relationships.

Some may have identified with Harry Houdini. He was a magician whose specialty was to escape anything with locks. To get publicity for his shows, he would enter a town and have the city police commissioner to lock him in jail where he would escape with ease. I know that my Uncle Cliff was insanely envious because he was always being thrown in jail for being intoxicated. He wished a million times that he could have been an escape artist like Houdini. Being like Houdini would never have worked for Cliff because when they threw him in jail, he was too drunk to escape and when he sobered up, he was too hungover. Some folks have no luck at all.

I doubt if many of our ancestors identified with Thomas Edison. This hard-nosed inventor and business man was the world's foremost inventor at the turn of the last century. He freaked some folks out by telling a reporter that he was working on a "spirit phone" to communicate with the dead. He later said, "It was only a joke." In my opinion, his being homeschooled didn't help to endear him to our folks either. You see, our folks were more into government education.

Edison had an unusual sense of humor. He hired Nikola Tesla to make his operational system of D.C. electric power more efficient. He offered Tesla $50,000 if he could update the system to make it profitable, and Tesla, being the genius that he was, completed the project in record time. So, Tesla marches into Edison's office and asks, "Where's my $50,000?"

"Tesla," replies Edison, "You don't understand our American sense of humor. I was only joking, but tell you what. Since you did such a wonderful job, I'm going to be big-hearted and give you a ten dollar a week raise."

Tesla got even. He went to work for George Westinghouse and with his Tesla Induction Electric Motor, AC current became the electricity of choice in the U.S., beating out Edison's D.C. Take that, Tom.

Our folks, I don't think, respected the super-rich. Those men like Andrew Carnegie, steel; John D. Rockefeller, railroads;

Cornelius Vanderbilt, shipping; J.P. Morgan, finance; and James Duke, tobacco and electric power; and other movers and shakers; didn't excite much pubic adulation because they were labeled "robber barons" by a slick, sensationalizing press. Our forefathers neither identified with nor admired these rich folks who would today be called jet-setters. Our people gleefully opted for a much more palatable entity that could professionally fleece the populace and put those amateur robber barons to shame. That entity was the government.

Now for some more local color. It is said that Henry Ford once visited Madison County and made this comment. He said, "A man who cuts his own firewood warms himself twice."

Zeb Vance once described Marshall as being a mile long, a street wide, and a sky high. Most folks who visit Marshall for the first time are surprised to learn that this observation is true; but, it doesn't include a chain holding a rock in place on the side of a mountain to keep it from crashing through the buildings below. Without the chain Marshall could be stoned at any minute, but perhaps too late for some residents who may already be stoned.

We had mules when I was growing up. They worked steadier and were easier to maintain than horses. Mules are ornery beasts of burden, and it was said that they would work steady and be dependable for a farmer for twenty years. When a farmer made the mistake of standing too close and directly behind the mule, it would reward the unwary, careless farmer. It would kick him to Kingdom Come.

- Arthritis, my great Aunt Bess used to say, is the meanest one of them ritis boys.

- My great Uncle Max was so old that when he was growing up there was no Hominy Valley in Buncombe County. He said they were just mixing lye with the corn.

- On one side of a cow's body two legs were shorter. That's because they were constantly circling in one direction around a steep mountain pasture.

- Potatoes were planted in a trough with a door at the bottom. The trough went up the side of a mountain and potatoes were planted inside it. In the fall all the farmer had to do to harvest the crop was to lift open the door and the potatoes would fall out the bottom.

When I was growing up, we didn't have a whole lot to wear. In summer we went barefoot, and my little Georgia tuxedo britches sometimes had holes in the knees and other places. I would be in the garden, and from a distance my older cousin would shout at me, and say, "You better get out of that tater patch, them taters got eyes and they can see you."

We planted corn up a mountainside by firing it from a shotgun. We piped the crop off the mountain and caught it in half gallon jars.

Mountain people were independent, rugged, and proud. They read The Bible, went to church, and paid their taxes. They are the only people I know with that much piety that would insert a matchstick inside their electric power meter to slow it down.

> A tourist asked a local whose monument (Vance) is that situated in the center of Asheville? "It's ours," replied the local.

> One day a balding Cody man asked barber Merle Stafford if he had anything to keep his hair in. Merle laid his comb and clippers aside and from a low shelf below the mirror he took out a box, and says, "Here, Clem, You can keep it in this shoebox."

> A new barber rented a chair from Merle. One of the new barber's first customers was my cousin Alex, a baldheaded man. He sat down for a trim in back and above the ears. The new barber rubbed his hand over Alex's sleek scalp, and says, "The top of your head feels almost like my wife's cheek."
> Alex reaches, feels his head, and replies, "By golly it does."

I'm sure most all of you have heard this one. So, if you've heard it, please don't give the punch line away.

> A neighbor boy Larry Kemp was planning to elope so he climbed a ladder and tapped on the girl's upstairs window.
> Roxie raised the window, and says, "Ssh, be quiet. You'll wake my dad."
> "Huh, your dad's not going to say anything," replies Larry. "Your ex-husband is holding the ladder."

You know jokes do change. That keeps them relevant with the changing times. By the way, that was the curve I wanted to throw you. The original joke had the girl's father holding the ladder.

Due to the dialect these must have originated locally:

> My Aunt Kate went to see the dentist. Dr. Sanders was proud of a new pneumatic device that blew debris from a drilled tooth. He blew on a tooth in her mouth, and asks, "Feel that air?"
> "Feel that air what?" asks Aunt Kate.

> My Uncle Max was stranded and stood beside his car on a mountain roadside. A game warden stepped out to the woods and suggested he put out flares. So, my uncle gathered two arms full of daisies and placed one on the front and one on the back bumper.

Marshall used to have a live nativity scene every year on the courthouse lawn. A lot of work went into getting costumes and live characters for the scene. One year a new resident questioned it. She wanted to know why the wise men were wearing fireman's helmets. She was informed by a local, who said, "Well, it's in The Bible."

The answer wasn't good enough for this new resident. She began to talk with some other new residents, and they went to see the mayor. He told them that the Reverend Kent was in charge and to go ask him. So, a group approached the Reverend. The leader asks, "Why are the wise men wearing fireman's helmets?"

"You Yankees never read The Bible," replies Reverend Kent. "It says that three wise men came from afar."

> After a night of carousing cousin Roscoe took Uncle Kyle home. In Kyle's bedroom Roscoe shined a flashlight against the ceiling and dared Kyle to climb the light.

> "Oh no!" cried Uncle Kyle, "I'd get halfway up and you'd cut the light off."

Once a tourist was camping in Hot Springs and asked game warden Monty Rainey if it was true that a bear wouldn't bother you if you carried a flashlight.

"It depends," replied Monty."

"Depends on what?" asked the camper.

"It depends on how fast you carry the flashlight," answered Monty.

One evening Cousin Roscoe was sprawled across three entire seats in Mars Theater in Mars Hill. An usher came by and noticing Roscoe, he whispered, "Sorry sir, but you're allowed only one seat." Roscoe just groaned.

"Sir," said the usher impatiently, "If you don't get up from there, I'll get the owner Mr. Owens." Roscoe just groaned.

The usher found Mr. Owens and they tried repeatedly to move Roscoe, but with no success. At last, they call the police.

The cop surveyed the situation, "All right buddy, what's your name?" he asked.

"Roscoe," my uncle moaned.

"Where you from Roscoe?"

In pain, Roscoe replies, "The balcony."

> Uncle Kyle and my Aunt Kate were riding along and having a knock-down drag-out argument turned screaming session. Finally, Uncle Kyle noticed a jackass over in a pasture beside the road. He asked bitterly, "A relative of yours?"
>
> "Yes. By marriage," she replies.

It was nearing Uncle Kyle and Aunt Kate's fiftieth wedding anniversary. One day Cousin Cindy asked Aunt Kate if she had ever thought of divorce. Aunt Kate replies: "Divorce never. Murder yes, but never divorce."

Uncle Kyle and Aunt Kate were at the hogpen one day. He was leaning against the edge of the pen when Kate wistfully recalled that next Saturday would mark their Golden Wedding Anniversary.
"Let's have a big party, Kyle. Why don't you kill a hog?" she said.
My uncle scratched his balding head, and replies, "Why should we take it out on a hog for something that happened fifty years ago?"

Kate, did you ever see a ham that good that wasn't from Virginia?

One day Uncle Kyle went to the doctor complaining of insomnia. After a thorough examination, the doctor said: "I can't find anything physically wrong with you. Listen, if you expect to cure your insomnia, you've got to stop taking your troubles to bed with you."

"But I can't, doc," my uncle replies. "My wife won't sleep alone."

A man goes to the doctor and the doctor says, "You're going to have to cut out wine and women."

"What about song, doc?" he asks.

"Sing only in moderation," relies the doctor.

One day an all bent over Kyle walked into the doctor's office. Opening the door to the examining room nurse Nora Wills says, "Walk this way."

"If I could walk that way," replies Uncle Kyle, "I wouldn't need to see a doctor."

Doc, at my age making love to a woman is an out of the body experience.

And just a year before, Uncle Kyle went into the doctor's office, and says: "You've got to help me, doc. I'm seventy-five years old and still chase women."

"If you're that old and still chase women, you don't need my help," replies Dr. Drake.

"Doggone it, I keep forgetting why I chase them," replies Uncle Kyle.

And just a week before that, Uncle Kyle was in Dr. Drake's office. He completed an examination, and said: "I can't find the cause for your complaints. Frankly, I think it's due to drinking."

"Let's do this, doc," replies Uncle Kyle, "Why don't I come back when you sober up?"

Uncle Kyle was becoming a real hypochondriac. He had diseases they hadn't discovered yet. He and Kate have a big house but live in three rooms because he stores his medications and pills in all the other rooms. He went to the doctor so much that he had his own reserved, private examining room. Uncle Kyle was such a regular patient that when his doctor went on vacation, he took Kyle with him. I'll never forget one day the doctor called my Aunt Kate. The doctor says, "Kyle didn't show up today, is he sick?"

Our neighbor Skip Carver was along in years and married a handsome young lady. Soon, the wife started to grow restless and fidgety and the marriage seemed to be in trouble. Dr. Parker advised Skip, by saying: "Your wife needs more affection. She needs lots of hugging, kissing, and loving. These young ones need cuddling even during the daytime."

"I'm working in the fields," replies Mr. Carver. "I can't be running back and forth all day to check on her. I'd never get anything done."

Dr. Parker thought a moment, and said: "Why don't you carry a shotgun with you. When you feel that you can put a smile on her face, pull the trigger and she'll come running to you."

About a month later Dr. Parker ran into Mr. Carver, and asked, "How did my plan work out for you?"

"It worked like a miracle the first week," replies skip. "Then the squirrel hunting season opened and I haven't seen hide or hair of her since."

> Saint Peter looked at a new arrival, checked his book, and says: "You're not supposed to be here for another sixteen years. Who was your doctor?"

EDUCATION

> My Cousin Connie returned from school and Aunt Kate asked her, "How was school today, Connie?"
>
> "It was good, mom" Connie replied. "We learned how to make babies."
>
> My aunt thought, "Oh no, the school system is at it again," and said: "Is that so? And uh, er, you learned how to make babies?"
>
> "Oh, it's easy Mom," replies Connie. "Just take away the y and add i,e, and s."

> Connie's teacher was telling her class about whales one day. "It is impossible for a whale, though large," she said, "to swallow a human because it has such a little throat."

Connie: "Jonah was swallowed by a whale."
Teacher; "I repeat, a whale can not possible swallow a human."
Connie: "When I get to heaven, I'll ask Jonah."
Teacher: "What if Jonah went to Hell?"
Connie: "Then you should ask him."

The teacher asked a kid right beside Connie, this question. "Jason, if you had a big apple and a little apple and you had to share with your brother, how would you do it?"
Jason replies, "Do you mean my older brother or my younger brother?"

MILITARY

I got to know Madison County draft board director, Millie Parker, quite well. One day she had this bit of wisdom to tell me when she said: "Maternity is a fact. Paternity can be a matter of opinion."

Millie told me about a tough old sergeant who was snarling at a private. The sergeant said, "I suppose after you get discharged from this man's army, you'll be waiting for me to die so you can come and spit on my grave."
"Not me, sarge," replies the private. "After I get out of the army, I'll never stand in line again."

I was in basic training at Fort Jackson in the 1960's. It was said that they were giving soldiers saltpeter to cool their ardor. You know, I think it's just now beginning to take effect.

LAWYERS, GOVERNMENT, POLITICIANS, AND ELECTIONS

> A local attorney became deathly ill. He went to the hospital and was placed in intensive care. His wife returned to Marshall and asked the local church congregation of two-hundred strong to pray for him. The preacher asked the worshipers to all pray aloud at the same time for the lawyer. You know, three actually prayed for his condition to improve.

A couple devised a test to determine their son's interest in a profession. On a hall stand they placed a hundred dollar bill on The Bible, and beside it they placed a pint of Jack Daniels Whiskey. When the son came home they reasoned, if he chose the money he would become a business man, The Bible he would become a preacher, and the bottle of whiskey he would become an alcoholic. They hid where they could observe him without their son seeing them.

He came in and stretched the bill, looked at it against the light, and stuck it in his pocket. He picked up The Bible, flipped through the pages, and tucked it under his arm. He then opened the bottle of whiskey, sniffed it, drank a big swallow, and placed it under his belt. He then went into his bedroom.

The father slapped his forehead with the palm of his hand, and said: "Lord, it's worse than I ever imagined."

"What do you mean, dear?" asked his wife.

"He's going to be a politician," replies the father.

We had a notorious local politician. He was forever being accused of inflating the vote count at polling precincts and was once stranded with the President and our governor during a blizzard at Wolf Laurel Resort. To get off the mountain and vacate the resort, there was only one snowmobile that would carry only one passenger. Our governor said that the President should get the snowmobile because he held the most important office, but our local politician objected and insisted they take a vote. You know, our local politician won the snowmobile by a three to two vote count. He even got two absentee votes.

> Our local political boss and a ward heeler had flashlights in a cemetery one night. The political boss flashed his light across a smooth tombstone with the name Mary Elizabeth Ward Smith.
> The boss says, "Look here Bob, we can make four names out of this one."

> I've met so many people who are defensive about our elections past. You know something, I agree with George Bernard Shaw, who said, "If you've got a skeleton in your closet, teach it to dance." In our case we should teach it to mark a ballot and vote.

> Heck, when I was growing up, our party won the elections regardless of how the vote went. It wasn't considered a fair election until it was rigged. I grew up thinking honest elections was a late Kentucky Derby scratch. You can't believe how stupid my dad and his side thought the opposing political party was. My family was so political that I grew up thinking that a mixed marriage was one between a republican and a democrat.

I started voting at an early age. As a youngster I voted in three presidential elections…and that was before the age of ten. Heck, I learned to mark a ballot before I learned to walk. Faux ballot boxes for switching were stored in old burley tobacco barns, and some of the election officials worked their tobacco crop early so they could gain easier access to those extra ballot boxes.

I remember one year there was a lot of confusion about those faux boxes at our polling precinct because our side forgot to dump the old ballots from the previous election and they got mixed with the ballots stuffed in the new election. Thanks to the cooperation from the poll watchers of the other party, our side kept switching ballot boxes around until they finally got it straightened out. It was touch and go there for a while. Isn't it nice when the two parties can work together in harmony like that?

Al, what I like about our democracy is that just about anybody is free to rig an election.

What about those old wives' tales where they paid a man ten bucks to buy his vote? Why would you buy a vote for ten bucks when you could, at no cost, stuff a whole ballot box? That buying votes was just a ploy to occupy the other side while the real action of stuffing and switching ballot boxes was taking place behind the scenes. Our side knew how to use psychology.

I dare say that I had the best civics education anyone in Madison County has ever received. During the day at my neighborhood school at Mars Hill, I learned that in America we have the greatest democracy on earth. At night at home I would mark ballots and stuff ballot boxes. At school I learned the theory of democracy, and at home I had hands on experience of how freedom really works. Wasn't that an ideal civics education?

Even years like 1960, 1962, 1964, etc., at our house were known as stuffing years. In December we stuffed the Christmas stockings, at Thanksgiving we stuffed the turkey, and in May and November we stuffed the ballot boxes. I looked forward to those even years.

Somehow, I feel that I was cheated in my childhood. On Election Day I only got one ballot to cast while the older kids got a whole handful. Sometimes life just doesn't seem fair.

Those old ballot boxes, those were the days. We were short of chairs at our house, so we little kids would use them to sit on. You could take the top off one of those old ballot boxes and use it for a basketball goal. Of course, you had to close the slot a little where the ballot went through to make shooting goals more like a real basketball hoop. They would hold four half gallon jars, you could use them for a waste can, store heavy metal junk, and when they wore out they made excellent kindling for the old Home Comfort wood cook stove. Those ballot boxes were handier than a Swiss Army Knife.

> When our election officials were caught stealing votes, know their excuse? They said, "Well, when the other side was in control, they stole votes too." That always puzzled me. If the other side was as stupid as our side said they were, how were they smart enough to fix and election? It didn't add up.

> When I was in the fifth grade, two kids were arguing at recess on the school playground. One says, "My dad can steal more votes than you dad."
> "Yeah," replies the other little boy, "but your dad cheats. He switches ballot boxes behind the scenes while my dad has to stuff them out in the open in front of everybody."

They say all good things must come to an end. The state board of elections investigated our primary election held in 1964. I suppose their theory was that you don't steal votes from candidates in your own party. Although the election results were overturned, none of our dear leaders were sent to the pokey. State law didn't cover inflating the vote count by stealing votes. So, in North Carolina it is okay to steal votes but not kisses, unless you are elected to office and sent to represent your district in Raleigh. That was some election in 1964.

Why, WOLS TV and the Asheville Citizen went nuts with negative coverage of our county. Had our dear leaders only known how to handle that mad dog press, nothing would have become of it and all that negative publicity could have been avoided. Yes sir, our strongman, as the media called him, could have painted himself in blackface, cried racist, and that TV pundit Bart Backsides would have been sideswiped and the whole matter would have been dropped like an over stuffed ballot box in the middle of the French Broad River at midnight. As they say, backward vision, or something like that is the best.

In my opinion we in Madison County got a bad rap over our elections. Just look at voting in the 2012 presidential election where in one northern inner city one candidate received 897,343 votes to his opponent's zero. Opposing poll watchers were forbidden to even enter the polling places to observe the election process where one-hundred-seven percent of the registered voters cast ballots and there was not even one whiny whimper from the side that failed to score. Sometimes I wonder if my old man wasn't right about the other side being so stone solid stupid. These inner city boys know how to hold elections, and they made out feeble attempts here in Madison County look like kindergarten play.

This blackface thing is the real deal because it works like a charm. Oh, had our dear leaders only known. I envy the civics education those inner-city kids are getting today. While they're electing state legislators, governors, congressmen, a Vice President and a President who are lawyers, lawyers, lawyers, a plagiarizer, and a community organizer, we were electing local candidates of whom one was a part-time Holy man, one was a traveling chicken peddler, and another was a full-time fiddle player. Shucks, I'd bet those inner-city boys would trade a sack full of lawyers and a community organizer to have gotten our fiddle player, and they don't even like fiddle music. Of course, they would probably want to keep the plagiarizer for the next election cycle. And no, we wouldn't have parted with our plucky chicken peddler either.

Yes, those inner city kids are learning far more than I did growing up. Today, kids in the rest of the country are ballot challenged by learning to vote only once while inner city kids are taught to flood the vote count so they can elect big, hotshot lawyers to top offices. It doesn't seem fair that they should get this kind of advantage over other kids, legal and illegal, in the rest of the country. To our truth manufacturing media, I'd yell discrimination and racism, but those are sacred words to be used only be a select few freedom loving folks for the common good under our free system of democratic self-government. Yes, my mother could shout I'm a monkey's uncle all day long, but when it comes to elections those inner city dudes are smarter than us bumpkin country rubes. Sorry mammy.

And there's another thing unique to Madison County, "Bloody" Madison. Where we got that moniker, I don't know. Some say it was derived from the Shelton Laurel Massacre that occurred during the War for Southern Independence, but after reading News-Record Digital one could easily see how the *Bloody* Madison label could have originated from the frequent murders that took place here. Maybe those frequent murders merely carried on a county tradition that began during the earlier mentioned war. Regardless, we're stuck with the moniker.

Ask me again, Yank, why they call this "Bloody" Madison, and I'll blow your darn fool head off.

These homicides were frequent. I was a little surprised to read that in 1925 or one of those years more people were killed in auto accidents than were murdered. I guess that was just a bad year for us.

One thing about our murders, they had nothing to do with clashing clans like the feuding Martins and McCoys. No sir, ours were equal opportunity shootings because you could get plugged by anybody and from any direction. I think our shootings had a lot to do with target practice. A gang of our fellows would be sitting around sipping some pretty good white stuff from a jar and one of them would suggest target practice. Then they would pull out their guns and start using one another for targets.

After high school lots of our Madison County boys entered the armed forces. When they returned from the service they used to tell war stories, but they stopped doing that because it became too embarrassing for them. I know Zeke Clay came back from the army and was showing the boys at Rice's Store a shrapnel scar on his left leg. Well, old Zeke felt bad when some of the local boys, sitting around the store, that had never been in service began to show him ugly scars, missing limbs, and numerous head injuries from gunshot wounds. Returning service men's stories were dwarfed by the local ones.

Shootings were rampant in Madison County. It was said that most Madison County mothers marched their high school graduate sons into the local draft board office to volunteer them for military service in the armed forces during World War II, the Korean War, and I'm told, World War I. In the military our Madison mothers believed their sons would be safe from gunfire. They felt that wartime military service would provide a safe haven for their sons. I believe that somebody exaggerated a little, don't you?

You're probably wondering why there was no gunplay at our polling places. Folks would go into their local polling place, and they were as well behaved as if they were in one of Reverend K.L. McKinney's church services. It was almost as if they couldn't wait to do their civic duty and get out of the old flourmill, greasy garage, or abandoned chicken house where the voting was taking place. I know my Uncle Rex seethed when the board of elections refused his offer to use his pigpen for a polling place. I guess the reason there were no homicides at polling places was that the other side was as mentally challenged as our side said they were. What a shame, those old polling places would have been bull's eye perfect for pistol practice.

> I had an African-American acquaintance who once told me that he wouldn't go into Madison County. He said that he didn't want to get shot.
> I said: "Heck Jerome, you're as safe in Madison as you would be in any other county. We're no more bigoted or racist than they are in, say Haywod, Yancey, Unicoi, Macon, Clay County, or any place else."
> He replies, "I know, but I'm afraid I might get hit by a stray bullet."

Lately, there's been a lot of talk about taking our guns, and they could. I hope they don't because if we can't use guns and have to kill each other with knives, somebody is going to get blood on their hands. Nobody wants blood on their hands.

I'm sure you've heard of sister cities. I don't know why somebody didn't suggest the idea of sister counties because we could have paired splendidly with Cook County, Illinois, that's Chicago. We don't have the large African-American population but blackface could have taken care of that. We had so much in common like elections and homicides; we were about equal in elections but there's a slight difference in homicides. In Chicago they threw their bodies into the lake, while here, our trigger pullers were nice enough to leave the bodies where they fell. That made work easier for out law enforcement challenged county.

Of course, we too have a body of water in Madison County. It's called the French Broad River that runs through the heart of the county and by two of our three incorporated towns, one of which is Marshall the county seat. Nobody would have dared to throw a dead body into our scenic river because anybody caught defiling our flowing rustic river water with a dead body would have been in hot water and in knee-deep trouble. Our river was reserved for important things like fishing, camping, rafting and dropping excessively stuffed ballot boxes.

There was a time when it was feared Cook County kids would grow up to be cross-eyed. That was from constantly looking down a gun barrel. In Cook County distances were measured in bomb throws, like, "Oh, I live just a bomb's throw from the loop." Or "I'm only a bomb's throw from the lake." Here in Madison we had our sayings too, like "I'm just a rifle shot from Hot Springs," or "I'm only a rifle shot from the Cocke County line." See how similar the two counties were?

Oh, a few minutes ago I mentioned expressions. No one in either Madison or Cook County used the expression "Over my dead body." No sir, if in either county a person had used that expression, somebody would have obliged him.

Our county and Cook were like twins. Goodness, in the 1950's I would have put our voting process up against Cook County in any election and in any year. Our political leaders used to say: "No need for a good ballot to go to waste. If the ballots are printed, we'll mark 'em and count 'em." In recent years I think Cook County has gotten the better of us with homicides. Our murder rate is way down, and we need to do something to improve it to get the numbers up. It's something to shoot for.

A stranger walks into House Appliance and asks Leon Parker if the town had a criminal lawyer.
Leon says, "We think we do, but to date nobody has been able to prove it."

My mother and my oldest brother were walking through a cemetery and pass a headstone with an inscription that reads, "Here lies a good man and an honest lawyer."
My brother asks, "Mommy, why did they bury two men in the same grave?"

Your honor, I'm curious. How does a sot lawyer become a sober judge?

The highway department had a crew working on a sideroad in Sandy Mush. The foreman, upon learning they had no shovels, called the office for instructions.
A highway department official said: "There are no more shovels. Tell the men to lean on each other."

Most government agencies offer early retirement. Get the job and that same day you start your retirement.

RELIGION

There always seemed to be errors in church bulletins. Here are some of the errors that fit into our humor heritage:

Don't let worry bog you down and kill you; let the church help.

New choir robes are badly needed, due to an increase of several new members and the deterioration of some older ones.

For those of you who have children and are unaware of it, we have a nursery in back.

Our sermon topic tonight will be "What is Hell?" Come early, get a good seat, and listen to our choir practice.

Our pastor is on vacation. Massages can be given to church secretary in the basement.

Remember in prayer all those folks who are sick of our church and community.

Members don't forget our church choir practice will be hell on Wednesday night.
Our new choir director invites anyone who enjoys sinning to join the adult choir.

This Thursday night, potluck supper. Prayer and medication will follow.

Don't forget our hayride this Saturday. Everybody, let's get on the wagon.

Overweight? Join our weight loss program every Tuesday evening. Use double doors in basement.

My Cousin Roscoe's son approached Reverend McKinney after Sunday service and told him that when he grew up he was going to give him lots of money.
Preacher McKinney says, "Gee son, that's very generous, but why do you say that?"
"Because my daddy says you're the poorest preacher we've ever had."

One Monday morning Reverend McKinney found a dead mule in the churchyard. He called the sheriff's department and was referred to the health department. He was informed that sanitation could not pick up the mule without authorization from the county manager. The preacher knew the manager and was not eager to call him because the manager was disagreeable and unreasonable. Or pastor dreaded the call and the county manager didn't disappoint.
He began to rant and rave, and finally said: "Why did you call me, anyway? Isn't it your job to bury the dead?"
Reverend McKinney paused, and replies, "Yes, Mr. King, it is my job to bury the dead, but sometimes I have to notify the next of kin."

> Reverend McKinney kept trying to get my Uncle Carl to attend church. My Aunt Clara went to services with their children every Sunday morning. She invited the preacher to dinner on a Friday evening, and Uncle Carl spiked the milk with some Old Crow Whiskey. After dinner the preacher without seeing her offered two thousand dollars for the cow.

> Preacher McKinney performed a wedding ceremony for Uncle Baxter. After the ceremony my uncle reached his hand into his overalls-pocket and asked Reverend McKinney what he owed him.
> "I never charge for the service," the reverend replied. "But you can pay me according to your bride's beauty."
> Uncle Baxter fished out a crisp dollar bill and reached it to the preacher. Reverend McKinney raised the bride's veil, took a look, and dug into his own pockets, and says, "Here's fifty cents change."

I was a member of a civic club in Elizabethton, Tennessee. In the club was a Methodist Minister K.N. Hennings who was saved at a Billy Graham crusade, and he told this story over and over. I think I know it by heart, and I know that he certainly did. He was invited to a Baptist revival meeting, and there was this man Harry Butts that for years the church members had been working with and praying for him to be saved. To everyone's surprise one particular evening, Mr. Butts was in attendance. The revival was at a fever pitch, and two women were praying with Harry to convince him to come forward down the aisle to the altar and be saved. At last they convinced him.

When the revival preacher saw the two women coming arm in arm with Harry down the aisle, he says: "Praise the Lord! Here comes two women with Harry Butts."

Reverend McKinney and a Methodist Minister were at a neighborhood picnic at Lake Julian. As they rowed out into the lake in one of the boats, the Methodist Minister stood up, stepped out of the boat, and walked over the water to the nearest stretch of land.

Reverend McKinney was astonished and decided to duplicate the miraculous feat. He stepped out of the boat into the water and promptly sank. They barely managed to get him safely to shore.

As his clothes were drying by a campfire and he was wrapped in a blanket, the Methodist Minister approached Reverend McKinney, and says: "You seem like a nice man and I like you. Tell you what, next time we're out here I'll show you where the rocks are."

> Constituent: Vote for you? Hah, I wouldn't vote for you if you were St. Peter himself.
> Candidate: If I were St. Peter, you couldn't vote for me. You wouldn't be in my district.

My Uncle Max

> My Uncle Max went to Ray Goodson to renew his auto insurance policy. When he finished renewing the auto insurance policy, Goodson convinced him to buy his first ever fire insurance policy on his house.
> My uncle asks, "So, if my house burns down tonight, what could I get?"
> Goodson replies, "Oh, I'd say about twenty years."

One morning a woman and her baby were boarding a bus. As she paid her fare, the driver said, "Lord, what a gosh awful ugly baby."

The woman was deeply hurt and found a seat across from my Uncle Max. He had to take the bus because his car broke down. He noticed that the woman was fuming. "What's wrong ma'am?" asked Max. "You look angry."

"That bus driver insulted me," she replied.

"You shouldn't take anything off him," said Max. "As a public employee he should respect you. If I were you I'd get his badge number and report him to the city manager."

"You're right, sir. I will report him," she replied.

"That's the spirit," says Max. "You go right on up there and get his badge number. I'll hold your monkey for you."

Uncle Max saw a neighbor boy walking with a lantern one evening, and asks, "Where are you going with that lantern, boy?"

"I'm going courting."

"When I was your age, I didn't need a lantern."

"Sure, and look what you got."

One day Uncle Max and Uncle Kyle were drinking in a bar when Max fell off the stool and landed in a dead faint on the floor. To the barkeeper, Uncle Kyle says: "That's what I like about Max. He knows when to quit."

My great Uncle Max went to an auction. He got caught up in bidding for a beautiful parrot. He was so caught up in trying to outbid for the bird that before he knew it, he had bid way more than he intended. He stopped bidding but it was too late. The parrot was his.

To the auctioneer, Uncle Max says, "Sure hope that pretty parrot can talk."

"Can he talk?" replies the auctioneer, "Who do you think kept bidding against you?"

One day great Uncle Max was observing two locals contracted to paint the flagpole for the town of Mars Hill. They were to be paid by the inch and were trying to figure how much to charge. A young coed from the college walked up and asked what they were doing.

"We're supposed to find the height of this flagpole, but we don't have a ladder," replied one of the men.

She borrowed a wrench from one of the laborers, loosened the bolts, and they laid the flagpole down. She then borrowed a tape and measured it.

"Nineteen feet, six inches," she says. She handed back the tape and walked away.

"Just like a woman," says one of the men, shaking his head. "We want the height and she gives us the length."

There's the college. Coach Anderson had a football player who made four F's and one D on his grade card. Coach Anderson says, "Son, I don't want to interfere with your study habits, but it looks like you're spending too much time on one subject."

Mental Health

When I was growing up, the neighbors thought you were crazy if you locked your doors at night. Now they think you're crazy if you don't.

A farmer was passing Broughton Mental Hospital with a wagonload of manure. A patient sees the farmer and calls through the fence. He asks, "Hey man, what have you got there?"
"A load of manure to put on my strawberries," replies the farmer.
"And I put cream and sugar on mine and they say I'm crazy," mumbles the patient.

Governor Kerr Scott was visiting Broughton Hospital and struck up a conversation with an inmate. After talking with the governor a few minutes, the inmate asks, "By the way, who are you?"
"Oh, I'm Governor Kerr Scott."
"Don't worry, these folks will take good care of you," replies the inmate, patting the governor on the back. "When I first came here, I thought I was Andrew Jackson."

Governor Sanford was visiting the same mental hospital, and an inmate asked him who he was. He replies, "Oh, I'm Governor Sanford."
The inmate says, "You are in bad shape, aren't you?"

After hearing that one of the patients in a mental hospital had saved another from a suicide attempt by pulling him from a bathtub, the director reviewed his file and called him into his office.

The director says: "Mr. Cole, your records and your heroic actions indicate you are ready to be discharged. I'm sorry that the man you saved from drowning later killed himself with a rope around his neck."

"Oh," replied the patient, "he didn't kill himself. I hung him up to dry."

By the way, if you live in Madison County and go to a shrink, people will start a rumor that you're crazy. The only time anybody in Madison County has any use for a shrink is to beat a murder rap.

My Uncle Mark was on death row in Raleigh. He and a Yankee inmate were called into the warden's office. The warden says: "Men, it is time for your execution. Are there any last requests?"

My Uncle Mark says, "Yes, I'd like for you to play the Kitty Wells song "It Wasn't God Who Made Honky Tonk Angels."

"That can be arranged. And what about you, Yank?"

"Execute me first."

A rich Yankee couple bought a million dollar house on Wolf Laurel. Their prize black poodle went missing, and they placed a two-thousand-dollar reward in the News-Record.

They were in Marshall later in the week and checked by the newspaper office.

"Have you had any news about our poodle?" the lady asks.

"No," replies the receptionist, "but for the last three days the editor has been out looking for it."

A traveling salesman's car broke down on a lonely country road, and he knocked on a farm house door.
A farmer answered the door, and the salesman says: "My car broke down. Could you possibly let me spend the night with you?"
"Yes," says the farmer, "but I'm afraid you'll have to sleep with my son."
"Oh, oh," the salesman replies, "I must be in the wrong joke."

My Mother's Jokes

Some mornings I wake up grouchy…and other mornings I just let him sleep.

Upon looking at a certain grave, she says, "Here lies the Truth because it never came out."

Her explanation for having such a large family was that she hoped that one of her children wouldn't turn out to be like the rest.

At the opera a woman to her date, whispers, "That soprano has such a large repertoire for one so young."
"You're absolutely right," he agrees. "And that dress she's wearing makes her look six times bigger."

A young maiden desperately wanted a husband. She was so desperate that late one evening she went out into

the woods, fell on her knees, and began to pray. "Dear Lord," she said, "please send me a husband."
In a nearby oak tree, an owl hooted, "Who-oo, who—oo."
"Anybody, Lord! Anybody," replies the young maiden.

My father's Jokes

A cosigner is a fool with a fountain pen.

A young lady comes home from her date rather sad. She says, "Mom, Jeff proposed to me an hour ago."
"Why are you so sad?" asks her mother.
"Because, mother, he doesn't believe there's a hell."
"Do you love him?" asks the mother.
"Yes, yes I do," she replies.
"If you love him, marry him," says the mother. "I think that between the two of us, we can convince him there's a hell."

Several men were in a bar. Two were arguing about the amount of control they had over their wives. Cousin Oscar said nothing.
After a while one of the men turned to him, and asked: "Well, how about you Oscar? What sort of control do you have over your wife?"
"I'll tell you fellows," replies Oscar. "Just the other night my wife came slowly crawling to me on her hands and knees."
With this profound statement a hush fell over the patrons, and they listened for more. One asks, "What happened?"

"She said, 'Come out from under that bed and fight like a man,'" replies Oscar.

An African-American girl was sweet on a small African-American boy. Her daddy decided that she was old enough to marry, so he called all the neighboring boys together to have a footrace with the winner getting her hand in marriage. The race was to be around a circular cornfield and back to the starting line. They gathered and then they were off. Soon, in a far turn the little girl saw that her favorite, the short boy, was lagging way behind. It was apparent that he wasn't going to win.
Suddenly she yells, "Cut through the corn patch Shorty!"

One Friday a husband spent the weekend partying, spent his paycheck, and never went home. Sunday evening he went home to face the music. His wife didn't disappoint and berated him for two hours.
At last she stopped nagging, and said, "How would you like it if you didn't see me for two or three days?"
"Well, that would be fine with me," he replied. Monday, Tuesday, and Wednesday he didn't see his wife. Come Thursday, the swelling went down just enough to where he could see her a little bit out of the corner of his left eye.

A doctor, engineer, and a lawyer were discussing the world's first profession. The doctor said it must have been a doctor because the world's first surgery was the taking of a rib from Adam and creating Eve, the first woman.

The engineer said that the world was created in six days from nothing. It was a major engineering feat to create a universe from utter chaos.

"And who do you fellows think created the chaos?" asks the lawyer.

A man went to see his doctor, and a neighbor asked him if the doctor found out what he had.

The man replies, "Almost, the bill was thirty-nine dollars and I had forty."

A man spent days trying to remember where he left his hat. He decided to go to church on Sunday, sit in the back pew, and during the sermon he would sneak out and take a hat from the rack by the front door.

He sat down and listened to a sermon on the Ten Commandments but instead of sneaking out and stealing a hat; he sat through the entire sermon. When the sermon was over he approached the preacher.

"Preacher," he says, "I came today to steal a hat to replace the one I lost. But after hearing your sermon, I changed my mind."

"Bless you, my good man," replies the preacher. "Was it when I started to preach 'Thou shalt not steal' that changed your heart?"

"No," replies the man. "It was when you started to preach on adultery that I remembered where I left my hat."

A man was told that he had a rare disease for which mother's milk is the only treatment. Luckily, the man's pastor recommended a wet nurse who could help him for a small fee. After about five minutes of the treatment, the wet nurse forgot her purpose and started to hear her hormones calling. She purred and whispers, "Can I offer you something else?"

"You wouldn't happen to have a Graham Cracker, would you," replies the man.

Two deputies came upon a horrible accident. There was a young man and a young woman in the car that was completely demolished. After the ambulance had taken the bodies away, two deputies began to investigate. A deputy spots a monkey is the bushes and to his partner, he says: "Sure wish that monkey could talk. He could tell us what happened."

The monkey moves his head up and down as if he understands. The deputy asks, "Did you see what happened?"

The monkey curls his lips and moves his hand toward them to indicate smoking. The deputy says, "They were smoking?"

The monkey nods his head, yes. The officer says, "Marijuana?" and the monkey nods yes. "What else?" asks the deputy.

The monkey looks skyward and raises his hand to indicate drinking. The deputy says, "They were drinking?"

The monkey moves his head up and down to indicate, yes. The deputy asks, "Anything else?"

The monkey puckers his lips to indicate kissing. The deputy says, "They were smoking, drinking, and kissing?"

The monkey nods yes. The deputy asks, "Well, who on earth was driving?"

The monkey begins to sputter through his lips and takes both hands to imitate turning a steering wheel.

In a local hospital a lawyer lay dying. His voice was hardly above a whisper when he called his law partner over to his bedside. He says: "I can't go to my Maker without telling you all I've done. I must confess. Do you remember that missing hundred-thousand-dollar contingency fee we received for a client from an insurance settlement? I stole it. Remember when someone told your wife that you were fooling around with our secretary? It was me.

And speaking of your wife, I was her lover for two years. In fact, she had a child by me. Then...."

His partner gently pats his hand, and says: "It's all right, I understand. You don't have to tell me anything else. I know everything. You see, I'm the one who poisoned you."

When I was growing up Scotsman jokes were quite common. Hear about the Scotsman who spilled his liquor on a hardwood floor, and it took him three months to pick the splinters out of his tongue?

A Scotsman takes a drink and places the bottle in his back pocket. He falls down on his backside and gets up, only to feel a liquid oozing down his leg.
He says, "Lord, let it be blood."

My father's friend used to say that he could spot a Baptist preacher a mile away. He's the fellow you see leaving a church member's house and picking chicken from his teeth while zipping up his pants.

Semi Urban Legend

An African-American in Mars Hill walked stooped over all his life. He died and Rayburn Funeral Home tried their best to straighten the man's back so that he would lie like a normal corpse in the casket. The man was poplar and on visitation night the funeral home was overflowing with family, friends, and visitors. Near the casket the man's preacher was heard, saying, "May this man rise on judgment day."

No sooner had the preacher uttered those words than the man bolted upright in the casket. It took the funeral home two months to repair the damage from people crashing through the storm doors, walls, and plate glass windows in their mad rush to escape. To lessen the cost of repairs, the carpenters used the new holes in the walls to make two extra doors and a large picture window. After that incident the funeral home had a completely remodeled look.

I mentioned earlier about Sheila Adams' book *Come Go Home With Me*. How many of you have heard that expression "Come go home with me," or "Won't you go home with us?" I can remember as a youngster that this expression was a staple of any visit. About ten minutes into any visit, the visitor would say, "Won't you go home with us?" Of course no one ever did, but it was the centerpiece of the visit and the remark was often made when the conversation began to wane. This expression was a local custom.

In the mountains some people can not say no. I have a niece who is an educator, and she was visiting a divorced educator friend who is a Yankee. When Carol started to leave, she says,

"Won't you go home with me?"

"Wait a minute, let me get my things together…and I'll have to dress my three kids and get them ready," replies my niece's friend.

Well, that lady and her three kids went home with Carol. They not only went home with her, but they didn't leave until six years later.

I could kick myself for asking this darn Yankee to go home with me.

Thank you for your patience. You've been a great audience. We have been a little long. I hope that you have gotten a few laughs and have a better understanding of where our humor came from and where it is going. Please note that, at least in my opinion, our local humor is deep and has been enriched by outside influences.

Outside influences on our humor tend to be metropolitan oriented. You see, that's where the money is, where the media is, where the performers and actors reside, and is addressed to a metropolitan audience. Our humor tends to be more in line with a short story. The packaged humor you hear is more of a one sentence variety, and I suppose it is directed to those with a short attention span. Maybe one line is all they can grasp. And yes, maybe one line is all the comedian can remember.

We appreciate humor of all types. We'll watch almost any comedian and laugh at his humor. But let me ask you, can you identify better with Bob Hope traveling the world, and saying, "I arrived in Paris but my luggage went to Brazil, my luggage has been to more places than I have," or can you identify more with a local, who says, "Shot my coon dog, Clem."

Clem asks, "Was he mad?"

The local replies, "He wasn't too happy about it."

Until about 1950 our country was about fifty-fifty urban to rural. Now, it's more like eighty percent urban to twenty percent rural. Our humor is wedded, I believe, to a more rural environment, and, to me at least, it is deeper, richer, and more humorous.

If anyone from Madison County ever does stand-up comedy, it might go something like this:

> Our preacher never preaches about tithing. He starved to death last week.
>
> ***Find a Grave on the Internet*** has taken all the fun out of our local elections. Now you can sit at your computer, never leave the house, and get extra names off tomb rocks.

We now have the best politicians that money can buy. Of course, that doesn't say much for the value of our money these days.

I have no complaint about the government. Ours is an economically challenged county with a lot of elderly people, and we're in a rural area. They helped to get a podiatrist in our small town. One day I was in his office, and asked, "Why did the government send us a foot doctor, doc?"
You know his reply? He says, "It's to help the old people in your county kick the bucket."

I've got an out-of-this-world uncle. That's because he stays higher than a kite.
The only thing higher than my uncle these days is taxes.

Uncle Max's old dog is so lazy that all he ever catches is the mange and fleas.

My niece dates a slow talking, soft spoken fellow. He's so slow talking and soft spoken that they call him a speakeasy.

I came for a small town. It's so small that the town drunk doubles as the mayor.

When I was growing up, our doctor didn't install a party line telephone. When he wanted to know the gossip, he held his stethoscope against his office window.

> The city council in a large neighboring city voted recently to cancel the circus. They didn't want their act to have any competition.

> When I came home one night, my wife could tell what was on my mind. She says, "Not tonight."
> "Another headache?" I asked.
> "No, a fever blister," she replied.
> I looked at her lips, and said, "I don't see any fever blister."
> "I do have a fever blister."
> "Where, show me," I said.
> She flips her hair behind her head, and says, "Look at the back of my neck."

Where I live is steep. In fact, you could say half the land is steep and the other half is straight up. We used to swing on grapevines for exercise, and it was also educational. One of the advantages of a large family is that you can use a younger brother or sister to test old grapevine swings. You see, in the summer you can have a swing that will take you way out to where you're a football field above the ground. A swing deteriorates rather quickly and by the next year you need someone to test it to make sure it's safe. That's when you recruit one of the younger children.

I recall one spring some of us kids were going through the fields and woods. There was a scent of honeysuckle in the air or maybe it was the odor of wild onions. At least there was the smell of something in the air when some of us younger children came upon a last year's grapevine swing that my older brother and cousin used. We had our five-year-old baby sister hold the vine real tight, and then we shoved her way out over a cliff to where the falcons fly. At the top of the arc it looked like a mile to the ground. You could see the tops of grown trees and the whole valley for miles, she was way out there.

We knew that if she returned the swing would be safe to use. This particular day we shoved her out there and she didn't come back. A minute ago I said it was educational. I will always remember what a bloodcurdling scream sounds like. And you know, I think she's still falling.

Looks like we'll need a new tester for our old grapevine swings.

Pardon me for exceeding in a couple of places the 1965 time frame that I set for myself. I believe I can be forgiven because I once attempted to be a politician. I had a condition known as Office Seeking Fever, which thankfully, the voters cured.

Thank you. Thank you for being a great audience. Thank you for your patience and allowing me to demonstrate what my wife has to endure. Again, thank you Madison County Genealogical Society. Thank you for your tolerance.

Afterword

It seems that humor is like a kaleidoscope. What is funny to one person may draw a yawn or a frown or even outrage from another. Humor, in my opinion, should gently rub but never scalp. Although my humor has sometimes been misunderstood, I have never attempted to use it to intentionally harm anyone. Anytime you have humor there must be a foil. An extreme way to express this is that if there is a murder, there has to be a victim. It saddens me that in today's society so many jokes are taken too seriously. If you want to be offended in this day and age, you don't have to look too far.

I'll admit that I've had a problem with jokes about women. For instance, in the mid 1960's I worked in an office where almost all the employees were women. A young woman was carrying her first child, and she brought to the office a small crib that had rockers. I walked into a room where this pregnant woman and a few other women were sitting. This woman was explaining that she could envision her husband, Mack, by taking his foot, could gently shake the baby in that little crib by rocking it back and forth. I knew that her husband liked to dance. Just like me, I said, "Mack always could 'shake that thing.'" At that time shake that thing referred to dancing.

I didn't think the remark was particularly funny. What made it funny was that this lady seethed for days and told everybody she saw about my inappropriate remark. Women would listen intently to her story and then laugh their heads off when they related her indignation to others. I suppose some of our best humor is the delayed reaction.

In *Tecker*, an unpublished novel of mine, I relate the following true story. It happened in 1983 when I was enrolled in a night carpentry course at a local technical college. There were several men and women taking the course, and one woman meticulously crafted a cedar chest that was thirty inches wide, fifty inches long, and twenty-two inches deep. It was a work of art.

This woman, I'll call her Jill, had a fellow student use his pickup to haul the finished chest to her apartment. As the driver and another male student were loading it into the bed of his pickup, to the student driver, I casually remarked, "I wonder if Jill would mind if I rode in the back and held her chest." I thought no more about it.

Sam, the driver, came back thirty minutes later, and says, "I told Jill what you said."

"Oh, no!" I replied, slapping my forehead.

He says, "Wait, I'm not finished yet. There's more. She says: 'What does he want to hold my chest for? Does he want to find out where I live?'"

I could have died. The following evening I thought I was going to die when into carpentry shop her lumberjack boyfriend came huffing to find me. I didn't intend to be mean. That was merely a private joke that had unintended consequences.

I am quite familiar with all jokes being taken seriously. Another instance and this true story happened on February 2, 1994. I was a democrat candidate for political office in a neighboring county.

When asked to speak a few words, I made the following remark to an assembled county democrat convention; I said: "Today is Ground Hog day. The First Lady went out on the White House lawn this morning and saw her shadow, the President."

I want you to know that the women in that convention assembly went totally bananas. All hell broke loose. I thought, "What in the world did I say? What is going on?" I thought they were going either throw me through a locked second story window or kick me out of the party.

I must admit that the joke wasn't particularly funny; but, I thought about never again telling another joke involving a woman. What a Ground Hog day that was!

That reception for my humor in the courthouse came as a shock. Only thirty years previously everyone in both parties laughed and joked about President Kennedy. Bob Hope told jokes that roasted politicians of both political persuasions. Things sure have changed from the time I was growing up.

As for my unsophisticated wit about women, I think I can be forgiven. I can be forgiven when my novel Mountain City Princess is published and you get to read it. Writing that novel gave me sensitivity training about the perils and pitfalls of a young woman reaching for the stars while she's breaking into country music. I know that you can't wait until a copy is available.

My outlook may be a little different than some of our nation's new arrivals. I grew up on a rugged mountain farm and my ancestors were Scotch Irish. These folks were rugged individualists that eked out an existence by raising crops in poor, thin soil. To keep them going through the hard times of trying to survive, these folks had a sense of humor as wide as the French Broad River at flood stage at Knoxville and as deep as Fontana lake in spring. When radio and TV came along, they gleefully absorbed the comedy acts they heard and saw. My ancestors' philosophy wasn't "anything for a laugh" but it was close. That is where I'm coming from, and I hope those who come after me never lose their desire to laugh.

I use strong sarcasm with Al Jolson. Stealing jokes and in intimidating the victim is an act that roils me. When I say *what's not to like about a guy like that*, what I'm really saying is that *I'm unhappy with him plagiarizing another person's material and then using legal muscle to intimidate*. In my opinion, if Jolson stole jokes and silenced the victim, that gives him, to my way of thinking, an S.O.B. title. By S.O.B. I mean son of a bloodsucker and I mean it as unconditional criticism, if those are the right words, of the highest order. Frankly, where is the fairness for this kind of filching?

I was a little hard on John Adams. My intention was to point out my understanding of his abrasive personality. I may have exaggerated his abrupt personality but that was to get my point across. Of course, John Adams was a great American.

Many of our county folks are defensive about out elections past and our county moniker. I believe that when you are stuck with something, you may as well enjoy it because change, in our situation, takes an eternity. So, we may as well laugh about it, accept it as part of our heritage, and use it for a tourist attraction. Today, I am more proud of my Madison County heritage than I have ever been.

Write a joke book without someone being offended? With the shifts in the nature of humor over the past sixty years, it would be difficult to keep pace with the shifts and not offend someone. As you can see, within the last fifty years, there has been a tectonic shift in what we consider to be humor. As a self-proclaimed humorist, I have been unable to adjust to all the shifts in humor as I painfully learned in 1994. Since 1994 I'm afraid that gap has widened and it seems that some people have adopted a Puritanical persona. It makes me wonder, have we become automatons?

In my opinion, folks should be more tolerant and understanding of poor struggling comedians. Let me add this. How would you like to be performing on stage and attempting to make an audience laugh when half of them are spaced out on alcohol, prescribed and non-prescribed drugs, or heaven knows what else? Being a comedian is not an easy task in today's society with all its diversity, ethnicity, and intolerance. In fact, the comic's job today is harder than it has ever been. So, we could be on the highway to where humor isn't tolerated at all. If we are on that highway, isn't it time we took inventory and veered off into a rest area? What would life be like without a little humor?

www.ingramcontent.com/pod-product-compliance
Lightning Source LLC
LaVergne TN
LVHW011351080426
835511LV00005B/238